TRAVELLERS' TALES
OF
OLD SINGAPORE

compiled by
Michael Wise
with Mun Him Wise

In Print

In Print Publishing is registered with the Publishers Licensing Society in the UK and the Copyright Clearance Center in the USA.

British Library Cataloguing in Publication Data: a catalogue record for this book is available from the British Library.

ISBN 1 873047 81 9

Cover print of Singapore waterfront 1848–49 by an unknown artist courtesy of Martyn Gregory Gallery, London.

Cover design by Russell Townsend
Additional pages for this edition typeset by MC Typeset Ltd
Printed by Utopia Press, Singapore

Originally published in Singapore by Times Books International
First published in this edition in 1996 by
In Print Publishing Ltd, 9 Beaufort Terrace, Brighton BN2 2SU, UK.
Tel: +44 (1273) 682836. Fax: +44 (1273) 620958.

MARLENE EVANS

CANCER:

My Enemy, My Friend

DEDICATION

This book is gratefully dedicated to those
who have supported Marlene Evans
these 13 years by word and by deed.

ACKNOWLEDGMENTS

THIS BOOK WOULD not have been possible without a team working closely together many hours for several weeks.

Beginning in 1982, Pat Hays Hehn typed many of Mrs. Evans' words about her cancer. Without these typed articles, much of this book could not have been written.

Carol Frye, Jane Grafton and Linda Stubblefield worked countless hours dictating, typesetting, and compiling the manuscript.

Rena Fish and Vicki Mitchell gave up time they had scheduled for other things to proofread this book.

April Cuozzo, Linda Flesher, Kris Grafton, Eva Lamboy, Cindy Lyon, Pat Phares, Norma Perritt, Sandy Rempel, and Kathy Wilkie did whatever needed to be done—answering the telephone, running errands, making deliveries, and so forth. Mike and Dorothy Dickson kept our temperamental computers in good working order!

Thanks to our family members—Dusty Frye (Carol's adorable Shih Tzu dog), Tom and Carissa Grafton, David, Melissa and Bethany Stubblefield—for sacrificing in order for this book to become a reality.

Many thanks also to David Stubblefield for helping to write the Introduction.

Of course, we thank our pastor and his wife, Dr. and Mrs. Jack Hyles, for the example they have been and for the opportunity to work in their ministry.

We are especially grateful to Dr. Wendell L. Evans, our boss as President of Hyles-Anderson College, for allowing this very personal look at Mrs. Evans to be shared in order to help others.

Lastly, we are grateful to every member of Mrs. Evans' family for sharing her with us and with the world.

TABLE OF CONTENTS

Part I
by Carol Frye

Part II
by Marlene Evans

Epilogue

FOREWORD

by Dr. Wendell Evans

I AM HIGHLY honored to write this foreword to my wife's newest book. When I fell in love with Miss Marlene Zugmier about 41 years ago, I had no idea that she would become a prolific author. This is her sixth book. Yet, the achievement of authorship is only one among her myriad of accomplishments. Marlene is a loving wife and mother, a college teacher, an editor, counselor and tremendous speaker. She is a conference director and an unfailing confidante.

She has three earned degrees and an honorary doctorate. Yet, she is as down to earth as she was when I watched her serve meals in her father's restaurant 41 years ago. She hates pretension, but she loves everyone. She is a modern "superwoman" and an old-fashioned Christian all wrapped up in one person. Marlene is so unselfish that it is almost impossible to keep anything extra in our house. I have to hide things or they are given away!

At the age of 62, Marlene Zugmier Evans is almost a legend among thousands of Bible-believing women in America. There are very few women in this country who serve God and love the King James Bible but what have heard her speak or held one of her many books in their hands. Far more people—both men and women—have avidly perused the pages of *Christian Womanhood*, the premier monthly publication which is available for Christian women today.

Yet, Marlene is probably one of the most underestimated women in the world! I suppose I'm not really an unprejudiced observer since I happen to be in love with the gal, but you must admit that I should know her quite well after 41 years!

I have encountered a few captivating personalities in my time: Dr. Bob Jones, Sr.; Dr. Bob Jones, Jr.; Dr. Lee Roberson; Dr. J. R. Faulkner and Dr. Jack Hyles. I have also seen politicians and entertainers such as Frank Sinatra, Jr.; Jesse Jackson; Harry Carey; Jack Kennedy; Richard Nixon; and a couple of Indiana governors. Now—let's be honest— Marlene did have a distinct advantage over those famous people. She's a lady! But, *what* a lady! When I first met Marlene in November of 1954, her personality puzzled me and left me a bit confused. But within a few months, I was under her spell! I hope this spell lasts another 41 years!

Years ago someone said that to brag on your mate is as vain as bragging on yourself. If so, I am incurably vain. I haven't even mentioned her tenacity through 25 years of back surgery, cancer, and pain. She knows the halls of the Mayo Clinic better than she knows the streets of our area.

Neither have I dealt with her strong character, her positive Scriptural outlook, nor her tremendous sense of humor! She is quite a lady, but if I don't quit writing, this foreword will be longer than the text of the book!

Lovingly,

Wendell Evans
President of Hyles-Anderson College
and the most fortunate husband in the world!

INTRODUCTION

by Linda Stubblefield

P ROBABLY ONE OF the most feared words in the world's vocabulary is "cancer." When a diagnosis of cancer comes, it seems like an automatic death sentence with the victim already on Death Row. Sometimes, it seems the word "cancer" may be even more frightening than the word, "hell," because cancer appears to be a living hell. Thus the reason for this book.

All of us who have had the privilege of knowing Marlene Evans have seen her accept her diagnosis of cancer as another stepping stone in life—another opportunity to learn more about life. Basically three of us (who work closely with Mrs. Evans) have worked on this book of courage which chronicles the two battles with cancer Marlene Evans has faced. At this writing, her second battle with cancer is ongoing.

This book was not Mrs. Evans' dream. Jane Grafton dreamed the dream of seeing a cancer book published by Marlene Evans. If she had not had this goal, I have no doubt the book would not have been written. What a loss this would have been to those battling cancer and other serious chronic illnesses. Jane spent numerous hours gathering the material for the manuscript. She worked many hours late into evenings to see the book come to fruition. Because of her motivation, *Cancer: My Enemy, My Friend* is a reality.

I believe among Mrs. Evans' team of workers, Carol Frye most exemplifies Mrs. Evans in her teaching abilities. Jane Grafton most emulates Mrs. Evans in how she talks to people. They were the perfect team to work on this manuscript. As I spent countless hours typesetting this volume with Jane sitting beside me, I often felt as though I were listening to Mrs. Evans.

Carol Frye wrote the Preface and the first nine chapters because, as Mrs. Evans' nurse, she "lived" the cancer with her. Recently Mrs. Evans wrote the following words about Carol for the singles column in *Christian Womanhood*. As Assistant Editor of *Christian Womanhood*, I am taking the liberty of sharing these words with you. Mrs. Evans writes it so much better than I ever could!

❦ • ❦ • ❦

Survivors Never Survive Alone

My friends and helpers have given me a lot of credit for being a survivor through degenerative disc operations, treatments, and all that goes with such as that. They've given me an almost embarrassing amount of praise for keeping on through 13 years of cancer operations, tests, treatments, and everything that goes with having cancer. I have to admit I like it. Even though I feel all that they say is not completely true, their encouraging words seem to breathe breath into me. Their words are like an emotional CPR procedure.

However, every time I am "pointed out" as the person for

INTRODUCTION

another cancer patient to emulate, I want to scream, "It's a team that has survived so far—**not** just me alone." I feel so sorry for people who have me "thrown up to them" without their hearing of the dozens of people in my support group.

One of those people in my support group is Carol Frye. She started working for me as a volunteer 22 years ago. Little by little she took on more responsibility as I had ideas I could not physically make happen. Because I was Dean of Women at Hyles-Anderson College, her volunteer work just naturally led her into being a dormitory supervisor and then Assistant Dean of Women. She lived in our dormitories for 17 years being on call 24 hours a day. The school grew and grew. She lived with hundreds of teenagers through their home-sicknesses, their learning the basics of the Christian life having in some cases just been saved, deaths of girls' parents when calls came in during the night, and all kinds of problems, joys and sorrows. I didn't give her much help during those first years, but she kept going.

Because I worked with the Activities' Department of the college, she spent hours and hours of her life planning activities for the whole student body. I cannot remember her ever going home for Thanksgiving or Christmas. As long as she lived in the dorms and as long as there were girls in the dorms who couldn't go home, she stayed on duty. Most activities and work opportunities at that time were right on the main campus, so the girls needed lots of choices for planned opportunities as breaks in the one main facility. She kept going.

I wanted fun for the girls. Carol sometimes teased that "my dreams were her nightmares!"

CANCER: MY ENEMY, MY FRIEND

During the 17 years she lived among thousands of dormitory girls, she, as a registered nurse, cared for me during times of more extreme "back-outs," her brother during his eight year struggle with Multiple Sclerosis, me with breast cancer, and both of her parents as they prepared for Heaven being struck with cancer at the same time. She kept going.

Now, I am not Dean of Women. Of course, I asked to be relieved of that responsibility with this last cancer flare up. That changed Carol's job, too. She has become an excellent classroom teacher who teaches all she learned and did in Activities, decorating, and helping people through hurts, sickness and death. And, oh, yes, she's being used to keep me going physically. She realizes immediately if I am crying a lot over nothing that I probably have an infection or I am experiencing back pain beyond endurance. She narrows it down, gives proper treatment, and makes appropriate appointments. I cannot tell the half.

Since Carol has no family member close enough to see what she has done or is doing, I felt led to write these words for her sake and yours. (I hope she will be pleased!)

Some of you reading this book may be single ladies. If you are, do you think no one sees you "keep going"? Do you wonder if your keeping on makes a difference? Carol does too—sometimes. Guess what? I feel that way sometimes, too. The devil wants us to feel that way. Let me encourage you to remember that God sees you as you keep on and just maybe someone else does, too!

❦ • ❦ • ❦

I believe God gave Carol Frye to Mrs. Evans *"for such a*

INTRODUCTION

time as this." (Esther 4:14b) I believe you can better understand from Mrs. Evans' words why it was so important for Carol to give an overview of the cancer years in Part I of this book. I trust the words penned on these pages will help you or someone you know or love face the enemy and see a friend.

PART I
by
Carol Frye

PREFACE

by Carol Frye

I N SEPTEMBER 1973, I was a 23-year-old registered nurse, studying to be a doctor. I was also a bus captain of a church bus route at East Main Baptist Church in Glenview, Illinois. Dr. and Mrs. Wendell Evans, with their two children, arrived at our church on Sunday for a speaking engagement. Dr. Evans spoke on "What Sin Are You a Slave to?" For several months, the Lord had been speaking to me about doing something for America. I was under conviction because I would help my patients at the hospital to recover from cancer, only for them to go home and die unsaved and go to Hell.

God allowed the Evanses to come into my life *"for such a time as this."* They asked me to come visit the college which I did the very next morning. I walked into Mrs. Evans' Christian Womanhood class where she was speaking on Philippians 4:4. She said, "You

Carol dressed for a Christmas party with Mrs. Evans

don't have to rejoice in divorce; you just have to rejoice in the Lord *through* the divorce. You don't have to rejoice in cancer; you just have to rejoice in the Lord *through* cancer."

I guess you could say God gave us an immediate rapport. I resigned medical school and became a Hyles-Anderson College student that day. I recognized in Mrs. Evans a very, very different woman. I often analyze what is so different about her.

Second Corinthians 3:2, 3 states, *"Ye are our epistle written in our hearts, known and read of all men: forasmuch as ye are manifestly declared to be the epistle of Christ ministered by us, written not with ink, but with the Spirit of the living God; not in tables of stone, but in fleshy tables of the heart."* Mrs. Evans' teachings are written in the hearts of thousands of women across America. The following are Bible philosophies regarding human relationships that set her apart and qualify her as an epistle.

1. **Marlene Evans accepts people and their idiosyncrasies unconditionally.** She has a love for all people from all walks of life with all types of problems.

2. **She has the ability to look at people in their individual circumstances and help them put their lives into perspective.**

3. **She does not try to control people or areas that are not hers to control.** Specifically I am thinking of the women who try to control their adult children. If she had given any indication that she wanted Joy to stay home from the mission field to care for her during this last bout with cancer, Joy would have done so. However, Mrs. Evans wants Brother Jeff

Ryder, her son-in-law, to fulfill his calling as a missionary to Papua New Guinea.

4. **Mrs. Evans makes much over little things and little victories.**

5. **She is continually aware of each and every individual around her and how to build that person.** This is not exclusive to her family. She is not a respecter of persons. She believes that it is her job to build and edify every Christian with whom she comes in contact.

6. **When counseling, she is able to see both sides of a situation.** She helps people see the assets and liabilities of their problem. She then goes on to teach them to emphasize the assets and forget about the liabilities.

7. **She is one of the few women I know who unreservedly gets the sleep and relaxation she needs.** She feels guilty when she **does not** take a nap.

8. **Mrs. Evans does not make a habit of displaying any negative thoughts she may have about her job, her family, her friends or her life.** In the 22 years I have known her, I have never heard her say **anything** negative about her husband, which is extremely rare in our society.

9. **I have never seen her question God or become angry with God over any of the diseases with which she has been diagnosed in the past 32 years.** I recently said to her, "You have had a life of pain for the last 30 years." She said to me, "But my first 30 years were pain-free."

10. **She does not tease or try to make points through**

teasing. She only builds others with positive comments.

11.   **When she counsels, she follows scriptural principles and applies verses to her relationships and the relationships of those around her.** For example, she always backs up and supports authority.

12.   **She rejoices with those who rejoice, and she sorrows with those who sorrow.** Recently, I spent a whole day by her side packing her back with ice packs after she experienced a very hard fall. The phone rang every 30 minutes or so, and I heard her end of the conversations. The calls came from Ohio, Montana, New York, Nebraska and the local area. It seems like everyone wants to tell her the great things and the hurtful things in their lives. I believe it is because she practices Romans 12:15 which says, *"Rejoice with them that do rejoice, and weep with them that weep."*

In conclusion, her life revolves around spiritual goals. She goes to every ladies' meeting and expects someone to get saved. She travels when tired in hopes of influencing one more life. She lives by a verse that she often quotes, Revelation 14:13, *"that they may rest from their labours; and their works do follow them."* This, of course, refers to the fact that she wants to live this life for eternal purposes. She **is** my epistle written in **my heart**.

CHAPTER ONE

THE PROVERBIAL
LUMP

MARLENE EVANS' JOURNEY into the land of cancer began in July of 1982. She had discovered the "proverbial lump" every woman fears and immediately called for an appointment to have it checked. Several days later as we left Dr. Cal Streeter's office, Mrs. Evans said to me, "Dr. Cal says, 'It's cancer until proven otherwise.' Let's go eat breakfast, Carol."

I stared at her unbelievingly with my eyes wide open. "Eat?! How can we go eat at a time like this?" I asked incredulously.

She grinned and said, "What? Do you think I'm going to stop eating just because I have cancer?"

I must admit that I had never seen a response such as hers to this type of earth-shattering news. A myriad of thoughts and questions immediately flooded my mind and minutes later as we sat across from each other in the booth at Zorba's Restaurant I asked uncertainly, "Mrs. Evans, aren't you going to ask 'why me?' "

CANCER: MY ENEMY, MY FRIEND

Her answer to this question was no less astonishing than her first response to the news of her cancer. "No! I am going to ask 'Why **not** me?' Just because I'm a Christian I can't get cancer?" she stated emphatically.

I was speechless for several minutes while I mentally digested this unexpected reply. Mrs. Evans has an unusual way with words. They often "stop us in our tracks," and her response that day left an indelible impression on my soul.

A few days later found us at Broadway Methodist Hospital where a modified radical mastectomy was performed by Dr. Dennis Streeter. Though I had nursed Mrs. Evans through many sicknesses, this was my first time to be with her during a hospital stay and surgery. It didn't take me long to realize that she was different than any patient I'd ever had. At a time when most people would be concerned for their own well being, I noticed that Mrs. Evans' main regard was for her family and how her diagnosis would affect their lives.

Her concern went so far as to making sure that the news of her cancer and surgery did not spoil her Aunt Lela's birthday party which was taking place the day of surgery. Aunt Lela, who had been like a second mother to Mrs. Evans, was having a big birthday party on August 6. Knowing how Aunt Lela cared about her, she swore us to secrecy until surgery was over, when she herself could call Aunt Lela and give reassurance in her own voice that she was just fine. Mrs. Evans, in a foggy voice—still showing the affects of the anesthesia—gave me the number so I could dial for her. I recall Mrs. Evans saying in an upbeat tone of voice, "Happy Birthday, Aunt Lela! Are all your friends there? I'm so glad you are having a much-deserved celebration!" She continued talking and then casually began to tell of her surgery. "I'm just feeling fine. I came through my surgery with no major problems...just a little mastectomy." They went on to converse for several moments about Aunt Lela's dog Mitzi who was a special guest at the party and other highlights of Aunt Lela's big day before saying good-bye.

I was amazed! In listening to Mrs. Evans talk with Aunt Lela, one would have thought she'd had "a minor surgery on the way to the grocery store!" Mrs. Evans had been trying to teach me that whatever you emphasize in your mind is the way life really is. She had said many times, "Look only on the good things and talk only of the good things." This was another opportunity for me to see her live some of her very favorite verses which she quotes and refers to often, *"Rejoice in the Lord alway: and again I say, Rejoice. Finally, brethren, whatsoever things are true, whatsoever things are honest, whatsoever things are just, whatsoever things are pure, whatsoever things are lovely, whatsoever things are of good report; if there be any virtue, and if there be any praise, think on these things."* (Philippians 4:4, 8)

Mrs. Evans chose to tell very few people about her cancer and the subsequent surgery until after the fact. Therefore, mainly family members came to be with her at the hospital. These included her husband, Dr. Wendell Evans; her children, Joy and David; and the Smith family, Doris (Mrs. Evans' sister), Jerry, Dianne and Mike.

Mrs. Evans asked me to make sure her room was inviting so that relatives who are uncomfortable in hospitals would feel welcome. "Inviting" meant having:
- a cooler with cokes
- a quilt for the bed to replace the sterile white blanket
- a throw rug for the floor

- all flower arrangements set artfully around the room
- cheery posters displayed on the walls
- a basket full of snacks for everyone to enjoy

A day or two later when a larger room with more windows and more space for people became available, Mrs. Evans chose to move—and so, of course, we moved all her paraphernalia with her to the larger room!

Mrs. Evans always says, "If you want the nurses in your room regularly, buy a case of coke and tell the nurses, 'Come and have one whenever you want!' " Such a patient I have never before—or since—encountered!

As a nurse, I had never cared for a patient who was so continually thoughtful of others. Her concern was for everyone else, not just for a few minutes here and there when it came to her mind, but all of the time. Mrs. Evans was *consumed* with putting others first.

The Evans' daughter, Joy, is a very inquisitive person who has a great interest in medicine. Therefore, it was natural that she had many questions concerning her mother's condition. Because I am a nurse, Mrs. Evans felt I could help Joy by answering her questions. Therefore, she asked me to take Joy to lunch the day of her surgery. While some mothers would be jealous and possessive, making them unable to point their daughters to other women who could be of help, Mrs. Evans is just the opposite. Times like these have not only produced a bond between Joy and me, but they have also strengthened the friendship the three of us enjoy.

Again, Mrs. Evans took time to make this happen the day of surgery. It amazed me how this woman could be going through such an emotionally traumatic circumstance all the while keeping her mind on each individual family member's need.

On the other hand, there were times Mrs. Evans *did* think of herself! One morning while still hospitalized, she called me quite early (6:00 a.m. to be exact) and said, "I cannot take any more yellow jello!" She continued by saying very seriously, "I flushed my breakfast down the commode. Please go to Bob Evans and get me one poached egg, 1 slice of bacon well-done, whole wheat toast with butter, orange juice and coffee."

One hour later I was walking through the hospital corridor trying to inconspicuously "bootleg" the breakfast to my friend. As I smuggled the food into the room, I said, "I can't believe you got me, the nurse, to do this!" We both giggled conspiratorially as she devoured her very favorite kind of breakfast. Word has it the plumbing at Broadway Methodist has never been the same!

During the five days she was in the hospital, I quite often found myself in the "catering business," delivering every type of meal from McDonalds' cheese quarter-pounders to cornish hens under glass deliciously prepared at Mrs. Evans' house.

Needless to say, nursing Mrs. Evans at her hospital bedside taught me a whole new way of handling a hospitalization. Allow me to share with you some observations and things I learned. I had no idea that I would be using all of these principles in a few short years as I nursed my brother Keith through Multiple Sclerosis and both of my parents through cancer.

- **It is a fruitless waste of precious time and energy to question God when circumstances or events occur in our lives that we are unable to change.** The faster we accept negative circumstances, the more quickly we can move on to the positive side of the situation.

- **If building people becomes a way of life, you will continue to do so during crisis times.**

- **Dispel apprehension and fears for others by using all the wonderful things God has put at our disposal.** For example, by placing a cooler of cokes in her room, Mrs. Evans added a festive atmosphere to the room and drew medical people to her.

- **Allow the people in your life to accept trauma the way in which they are able to accept it.** While some people want to know everything about their diagnosis, others would become very nervous upon hearing the details. Some people are gradualists and can handle just small amounts of information at a time. Instead of insisting on family members adapting to her way of thinking—to know everything, she adapted herself and her hospital room to those she loved.

CHAPTER TWO

FACING REALITY

B ECAUSE MRS. Evans' cancer had spread to her lymph nodes, chemotherapy was recommended. This led us to Mayo Clinic in Rochester, Minnesota, where doctors prescribed a six-month regimen of chemotherapy. Mrs. Evans asked many direct questions regarding her condition and her future because she wanted to know the full extent of what she was up against. In response to one of her questions, the oncologist cautioned Mrs. Evans, "We will be ecstatic if you live three to six years."

On the trip home from Mayo Clinic, Mrs. Evans planned her funeral and made a list of whom she wanted as her pall bearers. It was difficult for me to listen to this, but I could tell that she wanted me to reflect her feelings and let her grieve. As we traveled together through the Wisconsin countryside, the trip was a very sobering one. I understood that Mrs. Evans was thinking, praying and quietly making some very important personal decisions, one of which was to take chemotherapy.

Beginning in November of 1982, Mrs. Evans started her chemotherapy treatments, which consisted of three different drugs combined to kill cancer cells in the body. Because chemotherapy destroys *all* fast-growing cells, both cancer cells and other parts of the body made up of fast-growing cells in the body are also destroyed.

For example, hair grows a small amount every day so it is composed of fast-growing cells. Thus, we knew that Mrs. Evans' would lose her hair. The lining of the stomach, the tongue and the intestines are also made up of fast-growing cells. Therefore, nausea, vomiting, metallic taste in the mouth, and diarrhea were some of the other side effects of chemotherapy she was to experience.

Because cancer is a very complex disease to treat, there are many different drugs designed for various types of cancers. Cancer is a general term for more than 100 diseases characterized by the uncontrolled growth of abnormal cells in different parts of the body that can also spread to other parts of the body. There are very fast, medium, slow and slower growing cancers as far as growth categories. Each cancerous tumor is labeled with a *type*, a *grade* and a *stage*.

The *type* of cancer refers to what particular cell type the cancer is. For example, most people are acquainted with Hodgkins Disease which is a type of lymphoma. Along with this type there is also non-Hodgkins lymphoma, large-cell lymphoma, Burkitt's lymphoma, etc. A biopsy shows the type of cell from which the cancer comes. Sometimes this biopsy is not clear-cut because the cells are poorly differentiated—making it difficult to tell exactly what type of cell makes up the cancer. When this is the case, the pathologist relies on his knowledge and experience to determine exactly what type of cancer it is.

The grade and the stage are determined by the physician

at the time of surgery. The *stage* of the tumor is indicated by how many organs are involved. The more organs involved, the more serious the cancer. Hence, there are stages I, II, III and IV with IV being the most serious.

The *grade* of the tumor is defined by how much of each organ is diseased with cancer. So, based on the "big three"—type, grade and stage of the cancer—along with the patient's age and the condition of the patient's heart, lungs and liver, the advised regimen of chemotherapy is prescribed.

Often an inexperienced physician is not able to properly stage and type a cancer, which can be very detrimental in determining the best treatment for the patient. This is one of the main reasons why Mrs. Evans decided to go to a major medical center where experienced doctors are knowledgeable regarding the exact treatment of choice for each specific cancer.

Some could think that because Mrs. Evans looks only on the good and majors on the positive, she never really faces reality. Some shallow folks might think she walks around quoting Philippians 4:4 with her head in the clouds, not knowing what is really happening with her condition. I have observed quite the opposite to be the case. I find her to have a very keen mind for medicine. She always asks her doctors for the complete truth. Mrs. Evans has told me on several occasions that she wants to know as many facts as possible. She says, "Unless you know the truth, you cannot make the wisest decisions regarding treatment options." She also says, "Carol, God seems to give me wisdom to make right decisions when they need to be made. Once I face reality and make my decision, I then try to turn my attention to all the positives regarding the circumstances in which I am currently

33

living."

During Mrs. Evans' chemotherapy experience of 1982, there were no drugs available to completely control vomiting. Mrs. Evans has always said she had a strong stomach and expected not to vomit. She came home from her first chemo treatment and ate a healthy meal including delicious spinach lasagna prepared by Leslie Beaman. Dr. and Mrs. Evans were in the basement of their home enjoying Leslie's meal. I was upstairs when Doc walked calmly up the steps and, in his inimitable way of understating things, said, "Carol, Marlene needs you."

I wasn't alarmed because he was so calm. I made my way to the basement where I began running into "puddles" on the floor. I followed the puddles as my path to the bathroom where I found Mrs. Evans standing over the commode with spinach hanging out of her nose. She looked at me with surprise and said, "Carol, I guess my stomach isn't as strong as I thought!" We both chuckled but quickly realized we were up against an enemy much stronger than either of us had ever encountered—an enemy that no amount of mind control could conquer.

Due to the fact that she had a poorly differentiated adenocarcinoma of the breast, Stage II with lymph node involvement, Mrs. Evans was given three drugs—adriamycin, cytoxan, and 5-FU—every three weeks. The drugs were administered on a specific time schedule depending on how quickly Mrs. Evans' white blood cell counts returned to a level high enough to take another treatment.

She would take the chemo on Monday after teaching her classes and immediately go home to bed. As I mentioned previously, there were no drugs to control the sickness—at least in Mrs. Evans' case. Therefore, she was sick every 30 minutes to an hour day and night for 48 to 72 hours. She would then, very weakly, return to classes Wednesday or Thursday to try to teach.

Chemotherapy also usually affects the memory and the ability to choose words. I can recall many times standing outside the classroom door with a bucket while Mrs. Evans' assistant teacher, Mrs. JoJo Moffitt, helped her remember what she was trying to say by prompting her with key words. It was not uncommon for Mrs. Evans to come out the door into the hallway, get sick into the bucket and then return to class and continue teaching. I, frankly, was very astounded that she kept going and attempted to do the things she did during this time.

Because of trying to control the vomiting, the side effects from the medication made her hallucinate and talk like a drunk, caused confusion and depression, and slowed her thought processes. There were other side effects, but these seemed to be the worst. Needless to say, the next six months were the equivalent to, in Mrs. Evans' own words, "shades of hell."

One of the bright spots in the six months was one night when Mrs. Evans pointed under her bed and said, "Carol, there is a chicken under the bed!" She made me get on my hands and knees to double check to see if there really was a chicken under the bed!

Later we discovered that because she was wanting a piece of chicken to eat, her mind had confused these two facts. We have had a lot of laughter about "chickens under her bed"—

not at Mrs. Evans' expense, because she has joined in and encouraged us to laugh about it.

After telling Mrs. Evans about Brother Hyles' sermon one day, she later woke up from a nap slurring, "I neeeeeed toooo tellll Dr. Hyles the difference between a man and a woman." We are still laughing about this 13 years later. Needless to say, we did not attempt to get Brother Hyles on the phone for Mrs. Evans to give this explanation!

Many patients would be defensive and upset if these types of stories were told of them. But, unlike most women, Mrs. Evans has the confidence to laugh at herself and some of the silly things she does. Because she does laugh, she provokes those of us around her to be healthier and happier people. *"A merry heart doeth good like a medicine: but a broken spirit drieth the bones."* (Proverbs 17:22)

Mrs. Evans has always felt it best to do the following when you have cancer:

- Seek treatment at a major medical facility.

- If the cancer can be removed, have it removed.

- Research to find the recommended treatment by the experts in America for your disease. Call 1-800-4-CANCER to get free information about any cancer and the up-to-date treatment.

My observations:

- The primary care-giver of someone with cancer should

36

read up on the drugs the patient is taking, the possible side effects and what can be done.

- Take all the preventive measures you are able to take. For example, after much research, Mrs. Evans learned that a high percentage of women get cancer in the second breast. Therefore, she had a second mastectomy done as a preventive measure, which was a very brave decision. Doctors have since told us that this is probably the reason she lived 13 years before a recurrence of cancer.

- Don't sit and look at your scars! Mrs. Evans has said to me several times, "Carol, why do women sit and stare at their scars? I just don't look at mine. I'm going to turn my scars into stars!"

CHAPTER THREE

THE CHALLENGES OF CHEMOTHERAPY

A S I REFLECT back on those intense days of Mrs. Evans' chemotherapy, I also remember some lighter times. In December she and I were traveling home from California where we had spoken at a ladies' meeting. With a little coaxing, Mrs. Evans had purchased a hot pink Afro wig at a flea market where the pastor and his wife had taken us.

As the plane approached O'Hare Airport for landing, I said, "Mrs. Evans, why don't you lean over right here between the seats and switch wigs. Maybe the folks in O'Hare will think you dyed your hair for the holidays!" Now get the picture. She was nicely dressed in a conservative business suit with a feminine blouse, classy jewelry, nice pumps...and a hot pink Afro wig! As we walked off the plane, people began to chuckle and stare. As we continued walking through the airport, we received all sorts of responses and reactions.

Mrs. Evans loves all kinds of people, especially people with "soul." A tall thin black man with a big black Afro came up and said, "Sister, I really like your hair! Did you dye it in honor of the Christmas season?" We had a lot of laughs with that simple $10 wig.

Driving home from the airport, it was comical to observe people's reactions as they glanced over to our car and saw an elegantly-dressed lady with hot pink Afro hair. When we arrived at Mrs. Evans' house, we walked in together and looked up to see Dr. Evans at the top of the stairs with a very shocked expression on his face. He was quite taken back by Mrs. Evans' latest "do!"

He then chuckled and said, "Well, Marlene, if you can have some fun out of being bald, I'm all for it!" This was indicative of Dr. Evans' tremendous support of his wife during her difficult days of chemotherapy. He also offered to quit preaching out-of-town on the weekends if she wanted him to do so.

I remember Mrs. Evans saying so many times, "Why do women seem to make such a big deal out of losing their hair when it is going to grow back in a few months? I just don't understand why women go on and on about it when being bald is a temporary circumstance." One of the outstanding mental disciplines I have observed in my mentor is her philosophy of *stop thinking about what you can't do and get busy doing something you can do.* That is exactly what she did regarding her hair. Rather than getting all upset over the fact that she was going to be bald for a number of months, she simply bought several wigs including the hot pink Afro and had fun with them.

I have never seen Marlene Evans shed a tear over losing her hair or any of her body parts. I have seen her shed tears when she had to lie home in bed instead of going to teach because she was too weak from chemotherapy. I have seen her shed tears as she had to tell her husband and father the bad news about her cancer diagnosis, hurting for them and not for herself.

I have **never** seen Marlene Evans angry at God. No, not once! I have only seen her angry when someone is carelessly mistreated—like the time a psychiatrist made a thoughtless statement in front of my brother Keith who was an invalid with Multiple Sclerosis. The doctor said that Keith would never have an abstract thought again. Mrs. Evans was extremely upset with that doctor. She made a decision to help Keith dictate his life story, simply proving that the psychiatrist had bats in his belfry!

Mrs. Evans has told me many times that being angry at God is a waste of time and energy because when your mind is concentrating on anger at God, it cannot be focusing on solutions. She says so often, *"Get your mind off of the bad and onto the good. Get your mind off of what you can't do and onto what you can do!"*

I have never seen her question God as if to say, "I've been a pretty good person, God. Why is this happening to me?" From her lips have come no questions, no judgment of God and no anger at God. Instead she asks of herself, "How can I use what is happening to me to help others?" Little did I know as I observed her how much I would need this later when both of my parents would be diagnosed with cancer just weeks apart.

Perhaps one of the deadliest consequences about a devastating diagnosis like cancer is the frustration regarding daily activities caused to all of those involved. Most of us know that Marlene Evans is a rejoicing, fun-loving person who spends her life helping and teaching people. However, during the last several chemotherapy treatments and for many months afterward, she was very quiet and withdrawn from people. (Another side-effect of chemotherapy is that it weakens the immune system and causes its victims to feel negative and depressed.)

I have since asked Mrs. Evans what was going through her mind when she was quiet and withdrawn. She says she felt so bad, and everything looked so hopeless that if she were to have spoken, her conversation would have been filled with negative words. She says, "I liked nothing about life."

It amazes me that she had the self-control to stay quiet and say nothing. Those of us who want and love her influence on our lives with her good words are sad when she is quiet. However, I wonder what it would be like to be around a sick woman who complains all of the time. I find myself, when I have just a headache, wanting to tell people about it. I can't comprehend how she kept her mouth shut when she was so miserable, especially since she is a person who likes to talk so much. Truly, she lives the teaching of Philippians 2:14, *"Do all things without murmurings and disputings."*

When Mrs. Evans speaks of her chemotherapy time—two years including treatment and side effects—she says it's as if she lost those years.

Since her first battle with cancer, each time she felt sick with a headache or a backache, she was suspicious that the cancer had returned. She told me that she always believed she would have cancer again.

It's funny how Mrs. Evans can be so positive and yet so

realistic at the same time. She lives by the maxim of her old-time mentor, Dr. Bob Jones, Sr., "Expect the worst, but hope for the best."

Mrs. Evans always wants to know from the doctors what the worst is. She wants no surprises. She says she can plan her life better if she knows what the worst-case scenario might be. Armed with the facts of her disease, she then sets about doing God's will and helping every person she can as quickly as she can.

Chemotherapy is so damaging to the body that in some cases, after a certain dosage has been reached, the patient can never take the drug again. The drug builds up in the body, and permanent damage is possible. Each chemotherapy drug has many side effects, some from which the patient never recovers. For instance, Mrs. Evans took the drug adriamycin which is toxic to the heart. Mrs. Evans says that remembering people's names is still very difficult since her first chemotherapy regimen.

During the months of chemotherapy and for several years afterwards, there were parts of Mrs. Evans' job that were easier for her to perform. Those of us on her staff did as much of the work without her as we could. You can imagine the frustration for all involved during these years. I can only say "thank you" to our boss, Dr. Jack Hyles, for his patience in allowing Mrs. Evans to continue doing what she does best—which was teach.

I know Mrs. Evans feels deep gratitude to you, our readers, who went through some challenging years when maybe your subscription got sent to Alaska instead of North Carolina! It amazes me that *Christian Womanhood* lives on in spite of the several years when administrative details were so extremely difficult for Mrs. Evans and her staff.

From the time she finished her chemotherapy treatments, Mrs. Evans returned once a year to the cancer clinic in Merrillville, Indiana, for checkups to be sure the cancer had not returned. I remember wanting to celebrate her fifth anniversary of being cancer-free, but she wouldn't let me. She said, "I don't know how many times I have heard of some woman celebrating her fifth anniversary of being cancer-free, and then dying six or eight months later." Such was the case of Marvella Bayh, the late wife of Indiana's former governor, Birch Bayh, who died several months after celebrating her five-year anniversary of being cancer-free.

I always thought this somewhat strange since Mrs. Evans is such a positive person. But she feels better able to enjoy life knowing her enemy could well be approaching over the next horizon. Her life is characterized by Ephesians 5:16 which says, *"Redeeming the time, because the days are evil."*

When she made it to the ten-year mark, her oncologist in Merrillville, Indiana, checked her and then said, "Why are you still coming here to have checkups? You are considered cured."

We were both quite surprised by this statement, and Mrs. Evans never let herself believe it. Always in the back of her mind was the foreboding thought that she might have cancer someday again. Was the shadow of her adversary lurking close by?

CHAPTER FOUR

OVARIAN CANCER, STAGE IV

THE ENEMY DID rear its ugly head again during the spring of 1994. Mrs. Evans had been experiencing some miscellaneous symptoms such as heartburn, fatigue and pain in her legs. Because of these symptoms, she visited two different doctors, both of whom missed finding her ovarian cancer. This is not surprising since there is no foolproof test to diagnose ovarian cancer, often referred to as "the silent killer."

The second week of April, Mrs. Evans told me she could no longer handle the pain. I asked her to describe it to me, assuming it had something to do with the pain she has experienced for 30 years from degenerative disc disease and arthritis. However, after listening to her response, I was convinced her problem was something more than arthritis. I called Dr. Cal Streeter, and he immediately ordered an ultrasound of the abdomen.

A few hours later Mrs. Evans called me and said, "Dr. Cal told me to get to a surgeon because I have ascites; there is fluid in my abdomen."

I answered nothing. My heart had already jumped into my throat and then proceeded to "free fall" down to my stomach. Most every nurse knows that when fluid is present in the abdominal cavity, a very serious condition is the cause. And so...in a moment of time, I was thrust again into the fearful state of watching someone I love face a serious illness.

Mrs. Evans came to my office where we met with the head nurse of Hyles-Anderson College, Kris Grafton. We discussed the options and decided to have Kris call LaDonna Mourning at Mayo Clinic to see how soon Mrs. Evans could get an appointment with her physician there. Just a few hours later we were on our way to Mayo Clinic.

The next morning, April 14, 1994, found us sitting in the large waiting room on West 15, the floor where our physician of 13 years, Dr. Evan Frigas greeted Mrs. Evans. This was an unprecedented happening because the normal procedure is for a receptionist to go to a microphone, call the patient's name and take

Carol Frye and Mrs. Evans with Dr. Evan Frigas

the patient back to a private room to see the doctor. Dr. Frigas, Mrs. Evans and I rushed toward each other. It was as if he knew how very serious Mrs. Evans' condition was. Mrs. Evans was relieved to know that her case was now in the hands of her very trusted doctor and friend. We had a mini-reunion right there in the waiting room!

A week of tests followed showing that Mrs. Evans had ovarian cancer—with an impending surgery which would tell us more about the extent of the cancer. On April 15, we were in the underground tunnel that connected our motel with the Clinic. I started crying, grabbed Mrs. Evans and said, "I am so, so sorry!" Mrs. Evans was dry-eyed and said, "Carol, this is so unlike you to cry when you are taking care of me."

I quickly retorted, "I haven't switched into my 'nurse-mode' yet." (I have always tried to maintain a professional demeanor when nursing Mrs. Evans. I was trained in nursing school to not show personal emotions to my patients, and I try to do so when caring for her.)

Mrs. Evans was concerned that she contact her husband immediately. She felt it was vital that he be the first to know her diagnosis. She called Doc, who has been fighting the effects of no thyroid function and pernicious anemia for many years, and told him the news in a somewhat understated way.

The next phone call brought on a rash of tears. Before making the call she said, "I don't want to have to call Dad. When you are 80 years old, you don't like to think that your daughter is going to die before you do. I hate the thought that he, with his severe crippling arthritis, has to sit and think about my cancer." Mrs. Evans cried for quite a while about this. She finally dried her tears, picked up the phone and told her dad that she had cancer and that she would know more after surgery. It was a short phone call because she wanted to give him time to adjust to the seriousness of her diagnosis.

I took notice on how she talked to Mr. Zugmier. She told him enough facts for him to get the picture but minimized the emotions she was feeling. Again, I observed this unusual lady putting others' feelings above her own. *"Let each esteem other better than themselves."* (Philippians 2:3b)

Next came tearful phone calls to sisters Doris and Kathryn while Dr. Evans busily tried to reach their son David in Texas and their daughter Joy in the jungles of Papua New Guinea.

In the midst of this dark hour, Mrs. Evans retained her sense of humor. During a brief break in the phone calls, I said despairingly, "God is taking all my people away from me!"

Without hesitation, Mrs. Evans looked across the room at me with a twinkle in her eyes and said emphatically, "Yes, and I'm going to recommend that no one else become your people!" Her quick comeback made me laugh and lightened the effect of my selfish statement.

After her family members had been told the news, Mrs. Evans said, "Let's go treat ourselves to the Elizabethan Room." It is a very classy, restful restaurant near the Clinic with strolling musicians playing beautiful melodies.

I'll Plan My Funeral...Again!

Once we were seated at our table, Mrs. Evans said matter-of-factly, "I think I'll plan my funeral again." I pulled out a piece of paper because I didn't want to miss any of the things Mrs. Evans would say. (I can't tell you how many paper placemats I have in my possession with great principles and philosophies written on them that Mrs. Evans has "spouted" while we have been enjoying a meal together.) I was sure that this would be another one of those times.

OVARIAN CANCER, STAGE IV

I was still wiping tears from my eyes as we began to make a list of who her pallbearers would be. The waiter, a distinguished-looking young man dressed in a black tuxedo, looked at me rather strangely. I said, "My friend is planning her funeral." That statement caused him to then look at Mrs. Evans rather strangely! We both giggled. The people who work in the restaurants surrounding Mayo Clinic are used to patients and their special needs, but I doubt that many patrons ever tell that they are planning their funerals!

As I wrote names for pallbearers, we discovered that since the first time we had made this list back in 1982, most of her pallbearers had died—as in the case of my dad, Bud Frye, and long-time family friend, Art Tompkins. Mrs. Evans said with surprise, "Most of my pallbearers are already dead!"

I responded teasingly, "I don't know that it is a good thing to be on this list. Come to think of it, this looks more like a 'hit-list' than a pallbearer list!" I paused and then said, "So...who would you like to place on your new hit-list?!" We both laughed heartily.

After enjoying a delicious meal of grilled fish, rice and steamed vegetables, we returned to our room at the Clinic View Inn. Soon, very soon, phone calls began to come in from all over America. As Mrs. Evans would place the phone back in the cradle from one call, it would immediately ring again. Preachers, graduates, *Christian Womanhood* readers, friends and pastors' wives called to talk with Mrs. Evans. At the same time flower arrangements, plants, fruit baskets and balloon bouquets began arriving from wonderful friends all over the country.

As the flowers continued to arrive, Mrs. Evans then

became "concerned" that people would send so many flowers during this time that there would not be any sent for her funeral! She began to tease people and say, "I love your flowers, but don't think they take the place of sending them to my funeral. I want lots of flowers then too!"

It was quite comical watching the staff of the hotel as they made deliveries to our room. They frequently asked, "Who is this lady?" The employees at the switchboard were thrown for a loop because they could only put one call through at a time. The switchboard was "jammed" with calls for Marlene Evans.

In the midst of the many calls, Dr. Jack Hyles, our pastor at First Baptist Church of Hammond, Indiana, called and said teasingly, "If you'd quit gossiping on the phone I could get through!" This, of course, brought hearty laughter from Mrs. Evans. She has commented a number of times that Dr. Hyles' phone calls and humor were a highlight of that week. She told me, "Brother Hyles' phone calls couldn't take away the diagnosis of cancer, but they did cause me to feel very special, which lessened the pain of the diagnosis. It's truly amazing that being insulted by Brother Hyles can make you feel special, but it does! Somehow he builds you and encourages you at the same time he is teasing you."

In one of their phone conversations, Dr. Hyles asked Mrs. Evans, "Will you be taking chemotherapy?"

She answered hesitantly, "I don't know, Preacher. You know how that medicine makes me act so crazy!"

He quickly responded, "Marlene, don't blame the medicine! You were crazy long before you ever took chemotherapy!"

Mrs. Evans mentioned recently that Brother Hyles has coached her through the trying months of this cancer, especially through his sermons at church. However, these phone calls were the beginning of his coaching. Mrs. Evans had many reservations about taking chemotherapy for a second time. Brother Hyles' phone call and words of support were a major factor in her final decision to take chemotherapy again.

"Doc" and Mrs. Evans enjoying Bud and Bertha's company

With all the attention she was receiving, Mrs. Evans became quite euphoric. She said, "I feel like Tom Sawyer. I'm getting an opportunity to see my own funeral! Very few people ever have the chance to hear their friends express how they really feel about them. I had no idea that people would respond in this way!" All of this tremendous outpouring of love was a great cushion of support which helped her through the next several days of pre-surgery testing and doctors' appointments.

A number of people inquired as to why Mrs. Evans "went public" with the facts of her second cancer diagnosis. When I asked her about this, she said, "I decided after watching how your parents, (Bud and Bertha Frye) allowed their cancer to be used that I would, too. I learned a lot from watching the way they handled both of their diagnoses and deaths. The terrible sting of cancer was taken away because your parents used the 'C' word so often."

There is nothing wrong with praying for a complete healing for yourself or for someone you love. However, to never address the issue of death is to live in denial. When death does come, the family members who have been in denial are devastated. How much better it is to do as Bud and Bertha did in asking for God's will whether it be Heaven or healing.

By verbalizing the facts about your diagnosis, treatment and prognosis, you are helping everyone accept the difficult circumstances. You are also helping loved ones to grieve in a right way should death occur.

For the Christian, this is a difficult journey, but it has a glorious ending of hope. For the unsaved, denial is often a tool used to cope because they have no hope. How sad for Christians to allow themselves to live in denial as the world so often does!

Heaven!

One night I got up to get a drink of water. I glanced over to check on Mrs. Evans and noticed that she was awake. I asked, "What are you thinking about?"

She answered with a single word, "Heaven."

"Oh? What are you thinking about Heaven?" I questioned.

"Since I might go there soon, I'm getting used to the idea of living there," she responded.

OVARIAN CANCER, STAGE IV

I went back to bed with sobering thoughts about Mrs. Evans' possible death and the consequences her Homegoing would have on America and on our fundamental Baptist world.

Allow me to share some lessons I learned from Mrs. Evans' second diagnosis of cancer.

- **When bad news is received, do something "normal" for yourself as quickly as possible.** For example, anyone who knows Mrs. Evans knows she grew up working in a restaurant and enjoys them to this day. Therefore, after receiving the news of her cancer, she and I enjoyed a meal at a nice restaurant.

- **Laughter and tears are both emotional responses that relieve stress.** There are those who would think it strange and possibly even disrespectful to laugh during a crisis time such as the death of a loved one, or after hearing you have ovarian cancer, Stage IV. However, God gave us both tears and laughter to use appropriately during times of stress. Medical science supports the idea that a deep hearty laugh and a good long cry release certain chemicals (endomorphins) that are healing to the body and the emotions.

- **Real friends can laugh and cry together.** God often uses friends to give a devastated person support through the storm. A true friend will observe the needs of the grieving person and then, reflect them. During the 20 years Mrs. Evans has been my mentor, she has taught me how to reflect her as a friend. We have frequently switched roles through the years. She was my boss for 17 years, my counselor and mentor for 22 years, and my good friend for 15 of those years. I have been her student, her employee, her assistant and her nurse. The statement, "Familiarity breeds contempt," is not true about Marlene Evans. In spite of my "nursing" her, she still has my utmost respect.

- **Let people handle grief and bad news in their own way.** Reflect the person who has the trial rather than try to change them. A grieving person needs love, acceptance and encouragement, not correction.

CHAPTER FIVE

LOW-STRESS SURGERY

S URGERY WAS SCHEDULED for Thursday, April 21. The night before surgery, Mrs. Evans very carefully gave me a list of instructions on how to treat each visitor and make them feel welcome while she was under the effects of anesthesia. Mrs. Evans knew people would come to see how she was doing, and folks across the nation would be calling and want answers about her condition. She spent much time coaching me as to how I was to respond to each of the people who visited the hospital or called on the phone.

Mrs. Evans realized that I, as a nurse, of course, would want to protect her from too many visitors and phone calls in order that she would be able to heal more quickly. She wanted to be sure that in my effort to help her, I did not offend anyone or make them feel put-down. One of the last things she told me was, "Carol, as sick as I'll be, I will know if there are hurt people in my room. Since I am the patient and people's being hurt causes me stress, you need to be sure that there is no stress in my room so I can heal as quickly as possible."

Her goal was not just for there to be no hurt feelings. She wanted me to reflect her in my conversation by building and encouraging people who took the time to come to the hospital or call. Many of these people were some of her dearest friends, and she wanted to be sure they were treated properly.

Dr. Evans arrived in town the evening before Mrs. Evans' surgery. Thursday morning we were in her hospital room just before she left on the gurney. They hugged and kissed each other, after which we escorted her to the elevator. Her last words to me were, "Carol, don't forget, as sick as I'll be, I **will** know if there is tension in the room. I'm counting on you to see to it that visitors are well cared for."

I smiled and answered, "Yes, Ma'am!" while thinking, "Mrs. Evans is still 'the teacher' and still helping and building people and caring for others even as she faces her most serious surgery."

Dr. Evans and I returned to Mrs. Evans' room where I immediately got busy decorating the walls with posters and cards. Dr. Evans was talking when suddenly, in mid-sentence, his mouth dropped open in total astonishment. I turned to see why he looked so shocked and was stunned to see Dr. and Mrs. Jack Hyles standing in the doorway. They had come to see Mrs. Evans who, of course, was already in surgery.

Throughout the morning, a nurse from the surgical suite came every hour to give us an update on Mrs. Evans' condition. She would say something like, "Mrs. Evans is still in surgery. Things are going well. The doctor will be in to see you after her surgery is finished." Waiting for a report from the doctor could have been a very tense and nerve-wracking time. However, this was not the case with Dr. Hyles and Dr. Evans telling their latest jokes and bantering back and forth. Actually, a surprise visit from our pastor and his lovely wife made the time pass quickly for us.

After surgery we tried very hard to get pastoral visiting privileges for Dr. Hyles to visit Mrs. Evans in the recovery room but were unable to do so. The surgeon who performed her surgery, Dr. Tiffany Williams, came to the room where we were waiting and gave us a thorough report.

Dr. and Mrs. Jack Hyles at Methodist Hospital

Dr. Williams, a tall, lanky, bearded man with 35 years of experience in dealing with gynecological cancers, told us that he was able to remove 96 percent of the cancer. The surgery was quite extensive and included removing several organs, a tumor the size of a large cantaloupe, the omentum (the protective covering lining the abdominal cavity), and scraping her abdomen in an attempt to remove as much cancer as possible. He was as positive as he could be about the results, but he did not give us unrealistic expectations for Mrs. Evans' prognosis.

Unfortunately for Mrs. Evans, Dr. and Mrs. Hyles had to return home before she came back to her hospital room. However, their visit was a great support to Dr. Evans. He later said in awe, "It's unbelievable that Brother and Mrs. Hyles would take a whole day to fly to Minnesota just to be here for Marlene and me when he spends so much of his life in airports and on planes!" In fact, they flew back to O'Hare that evening only to return at 5:00 the next morning when Dr. Hyles drove Mrs. Hyles to the airport so she could fly to a ladies' conference.

Mrs. Evans returned to the room from recovery several hours later, still somewhat groggy and in quite a bit of pain. As I have cared for Mrs. Evans through these years, I often tell her that she is the easiest patient I have ever taken care of because she doesn't complain. She also follows instructions implicitly which is a significant factor in getting well after surgery. Learning how to handle body movements properly also promotes the healing process. For example, just the way a patient gets in and out of bed can determine the amount of strain put on the incision. Mrs. Evans immediately had me teach her the proper techniques of getting up and down and in and out of bed.

Also, it is important to begin walking very soon after most surgeries to prevent blood clots, pneumonia and other possible complications of surgery. And so, Mrs. Evans began taking walks around the nurses' station without delay once she was directed to do so. In fact, she was so obedient that the nurses had to slow her down!

In order to give me some relief, Jane Grafton, Linda Stubblefield and Vicki Mitchell came for the weekend. We each took shifts caring for Mrs. Evans, her visitors, her telephone calls and her flowers. Mrs. Evans does not like *anything* dead so every dead leaf, petal or flower was to be immediately plucked from each arrangement. We almost needed a full-time gardener just to care for the plants and flowers!

LOW-STRESS SURGERY

Two spiral notebooks were kept in the room. The first included a notation regarding every gift and every visitor so Mrs. Evans could keep track of this information. The second was a journal which included information about Mrs. Evans' condition, instructions for the care givers who stayed with her and other special details that were pertinent to her care.

Several nights the person "on duty" slept in the chair next to Mrs. Evans' bed and pushed the button on the morphine pump machine to help keep her pain under control. Mrs. Evans used these times alone with people to encourage them, counsel them and help them in any way she could. It was a life-changing time as Linda Stubblefield will be telling in the following chapter. It seems amazing to me that Mrs. Evans could counsel and help others in her extremely weakened condition.

As a nurse, my natural thought was that Mrs. Evans should not be caring for others, only for herself in order for her to recover as quickly as possible. And yet, God seems to use Mrs. Evans and give her the extra strength necessary to help others during these times.

Mrs. Evans was in the hospital for a week and then returned home April 29. I had to fly from Rochester to Flint, Michigan, to speak at a ladies' meeting where she had been scheduled. Because of her condition, I did not want to leave her. Consequently her good friends, Skip and Bev Buskoll, who live near Minneapolis, Minnesota, graciously offered to drive her to Indiana. They drove only as many miles in a day as Mrs. Evans could take and then went to a motel for the night. They made the trip as easy and as comfortable as possible for her.

CANCER: MY ENEMY, MY FRIEND

We were home two weeks when Mayo Clinic called for us to return. Because of the seriousness of Mrs. Evans' cancer, the doctors wanted to begin chemotherapy three weeks after surgery. We drove to Minnesota, but due to complications with the healing of Mrs. Evans' incision, Dr. Hartman delayed treatment for another two weeks.

On our next visit Dr. Lynn Hartman, the oncology expert for ovarian cancer at Mayo Clinic, answered many of our questions. When Mrs. Evans asked, "What is the natural course for this disease?" Dr. Hartman answered, "Studies show that women with ovarian cancer, Stage IV usually live two to five years after diagnosis. The devilish nature of this disease is that it will come back in full force eighteen months after diagnosis." Mrs. Evans took in all of the information very matter-of-factly.

I will never forget our trip home from Mayo. We listened to a sermon by Brother Hyles entitled, *May I Please Change Seats?* He told how he didn't like his assigned seat on a particular flight. However, he was unable to move to another. During the sermon, he referred to Mrs. Evans' cancer and how she is now sitting in a seat that she cannot change. This message was a great encouragement to both of us. (This same sermon was a source of great help and encouragement to Joy Evans Ryder just a few months later.)

We arrived in the Chicago area, and immediately we were in bumper-to-bumper, on-the-brakes traffic. Mrs. Evans was reclining in the front seat to take the pressure off of her incision. Because we had been in the car for six hours, we were both a little "antsy," so, I put on a gospel quartet tape to bring some life to two weary travelers. Soon Mrs. Evans began leading the music with one hand, snapping her fingers with the other, and tapping her feet. We joined the vocalists in our own rendition of "Beulah Land." I began crying— thinking of her going to Heaven—but did not want her to see me.

She noticed my tears (You can't hide too much from her for too long!) and asked why I was crying. I answered, "You do so much good on this earth by building people, and I just can't picture life without your being here."

She replied with a mischievous grin, "Don't worry, Carol. I'll be here a long time yet keeping all you kids out of trouble!" (She lovingly refers to her staff members—all of us ladies over forty—as kids, and we love it!)

I was afraid that my tears would hurt the spirit of joyfulness we had been sharing. However, a few minutes later I glanced over to see her still smiling and "directing" her own miniature orchestra!

CHAPTER SIX

A WRONG FOCUS

O NE OF MRS. Evans' greatest strengths is that, in spite of her outgoing personality, when she counsels she never divulges the information of that conference with anyone. Because she counsels many of us who are friends and co-workers, outsiders might assume that she shares confidentialities.

Completely unbeknownst to me, Linda Stubblefield had refused to take counsel or teaching from Mrs. Evans. A few weeks before her cancer diagnosis when I went to Mrs. Evans for counsel, she was very hesitant to answer my questions. She said that she felt she had hurt herself permanently with someone by giving correction, and she didn't want to make the same mistake again.

Because I have found myself lacking in several human relationship skills, Mrs. Evans has been working with me for several years. Her acting so hesitant with me and almost forcing me to drag the advice I needed from her, when she had been answering my questions without hesitation for years was confusing to me. (Linda has since told me that she was that "someone".)

CANCER: MY ENEMY, MY FRIEND

James 5:16a says, *"Confess your faults one to another, and pray for one another, that ye may be healed."* I had no idea what all had occurred between Linda and Mrs. Evans through the years, but I do know that when people are honest and practice James 5:16, lives are changed. Since the minute she heard the diagnosis, Linda has practiced confessing her faults. Those of us who know her and love her have seen a dynamic change in her life. Therefore, I have asked her to share her heart in this chapter regarding Mrs. Evans' cancer diagnosis.

❦ • ❦ • ❦

When I left Pennsylvania in 1974 to attend Hyles-Anderson College, I left behind many things—my parents, four sisters and two brothers, the college from which I had hoped to graduate, an excellent job opportunity already offered by the school that would be my alma mater, all my friends of 19 years and my church.

However, there was one thing I didn't leave behind — my wrong focus. I brought with me some unresolved conflicts with an important person in my life. When I arrived at Hyles-Anderson College, that focus promptly moved. My new focus? Marlene Evans.

I am unable to explain all the workings and machinations of the human mind, but when my focus changed to Mrs. Evans, my feelings of antipathy and conflict moved also. New battle lines were drawn inwardly.

In order to help me through these conflicts, Mrs. Evans hired me as a student secretary. When I finished my degree in January 1977, she hired me to work with *Christian*

Womanhood. (She's a glutton for punishment!) As she tried
to teach me and tried to retrain my thinking, I fought and
seethed inwardly. She reminded me so much of the person
with whom I had never resolved some personal conflicts. The
hostility grew and grew to the point where I hated attending
her meetings and hearing her speak. I am embarrassed to
admit that if I felt I could have gotten away with it, I would
have stayed home from the nationwide *Christian Womanhood*
Spectacular every October.

That is not to say that we didn't have some good times.
Most of the time, Mrs. Evans never knew how inwardly
angry I was. Eventually though, my hostility became more
outward; at this point, we tried not to work closely together.
I performed my work requirements, sent the work for
approval and received replies. Occasionally, we worked via
the telephone. We both drew our perimeters and stayed within
our "safe zones."

In the spring of 1994, Dr. Jack Schaap preached a classic
sermon in college chapel entitled "The Polished Shaft"
showing how God can use an imperfect arrow. Immediately
after that message Mrs. Evans asked me to come to her
office. It was obvious to me she was deeply touched by his
message as she started talking with me about our relationship
and my future. Though she said many kind things, **all** I heard
her say was, "You will never be anything for God" which she
did not say at all. I heard nothing else she said beyond that
point.

I can still remember thinking, "I have done so much for
you. How much more do you want? How much do I have to
do to make you happy? That's it. You will never hurt me
again." I stood and said, "I have an appointment. I need to go

because the person is waiting in her car." When I physically closed the door of Mrs. Evans' office behind me, I emotionally shut the door of my heart.

About two weeks later, I came home to a message on my answering machine from Mrs. Evans. She was calling to let me know that she was leaving immediately for Mayo Clinic. I sarcastically thought, "Yeah, there you go again—off to Mayo."

Two days later, I somehow knew that I needed to reach her. However, I was unable to get a telephone number. So I tried to put aside the feeling of foreboding.

The next morning my husband and I were getting ready to go calling on our church bus route. We couldn't seem to get out the door at our regular time and just as we were about to leave (an hour later than usual), the phone rang. My husband answered (thinking we would leave more quickly if he took the call), and I heard him say, "No, she's not available; she's already married." He laughed, handed me the phone and said, "It's Mrs. Evans."

After I said, "Hello," she said, "Linda, have you heard about my diagnosis?"

"No," I answered abruptly.

"It's cancer."

"This is because of me!" I cried. I heard her sob and the sound of her phone dropping as I laid my head on my desk and began to weep uncontrollably. I then heard another voice on the phone, "Linda, this is Carol. Mrs. Evans is crying, and she can't talk. Let me tell you about her diagnosis."

Carol quietly told me the facts while both Mrs. Evans and I tried to calm ourselves. When Mrs. Evans finally came back on the line, I said, "Don't say anything. I have some things I must say to you first. I have been cold, hard-hearted and stiff-necked. I have refused to listen and learn from you. God allowed you to have this cancer because I wouldn't change. It's all because of me."

Mrs. Evans replied with understanding and grace, "I don't know what His reasons are. I just feel so badly that I'm not going to be here to help you through this."

Mrs. Evans was scheduled for major surgery five days later. During those five days, I had major surgery done on my heart. I discovered how very much I cared about her—so much so that I did something I have never done in my life. I withdrew some money from our savings account, got in a car with Jane Grafton and drove to Mayo Clinic. I felt as though I would never see Mrs. Evans alive again, and I knew I had to get things right with her.

When we arrived at the hospital less than 24 hours after her surgery, Jane and I could see Mrs. Evans lying on her hospital bed—deathly white with tubes everywhere. When Carol told her we were there, we walked in to find her standing with her arms open wide to receive us. I believe I know how the prodigal son must have felt when he came home, only I was away for 19 years.

That night I sat beside her hospital bed, and we talked into the early hours of the morning. We didn't talk about all the hurts and problems that had distanced us in the past. We simply made plans to go forward for however long we had together. We both cried, we both struggled for the right words, and for the first time in 39 years, my focus changed. The hurts were finally put aside and forgotten.

As I look back to April 1994, I believe I was given a reprieve to make up for the hurts and anxiety I had caused Mrs. Evans during the years I worked with her. I was given a reprieve to give her the best of me for the rest of our lives together.

Some of you who are reading this book are like I was. Your focus has been wrong. You remain so tied to the memories of hurts in the past that you refuse to let God heal. You do what I did. You transfer that focus to someone (who doesn't deserve it) who reminds you of the one who hurt you in the past.

The following is a list of some of the lessons I learned from this experience.

• I learned that I had robbed my co-workers of having the best from Mrs. Evans. I wrote to each of them asking for their forgiveness.

• I learned that I had robbed Mrs. Evans' family of having her best. I wrote to Dr. Evans and asked for his forgiveness. I would like to share a part of his answer with you that has been a tremendous help to me in the days and months following my decision.

Thank you so much for your letter of April 24. Of course, forgiveness is no problem at all. I appreciate so much the spirit of your letter, and I rejoice in the decisions that you are making, and I hear good reports on the manner in which you are following up those decisions. Thank you so much for all of your hard work for Mrs. Evans and for Christian Womanhood. You are a very talented and intelligent lady. Now, as you mature into a new phase of your relationships with people, Satan will tempt you many many times to go back to your old ways. I urge you to resist his blandishments with all your might.

• I called some people on the telephone with whom I knew I was not right and asked forgiveness.

• I learned that when I would say something hurtful to a person, I needed to go to that person *immediately* and ask forgiveness.

• I learned that I needed to "clear the air" when misunderstandings occurred. In the past, I let things build up to a boiling point, and then I would explode.

• I realized that I had robbed myself of many years of one-on-one teaching from Mrs. Evans. I can never recapture the opportunities I missed, but I can, from this point on, take correction and teaching from her with a right spirit every opportunity I get.

• I learned that I had "selective hearing." Allow me to call it that for lack of a better term. When Mrs. Evans asked me to come to her office the day Brother Schaap preached the "Polished Shaft" message, I did not hear all the good statements she made. I heard only the negative and that incorrectly. I have learned that I must retrain myself to hear *every* word someone is saying to me.

CANCER: MY ENEMY, MY FRIEND

- I believe the greatest thing I learned to do was pray every day, many times a day for Mrs. Evans.

I'm sure there are other lessons I learned and am still learning. These eight stand out most in my mind. It has not been easy. I still have times of wanting to "close the door." I still make remarks for which I have to ask forgiveness. It is much easier to live a stagnant life with no growth and no change. When a person changes, he is admitting that he has been wrong. I've yet to meet a person who likes to admit he's been wrong!

Recently I asked Mrs. Evans why she continued to keep me as an employee when I was so obviously "upsetting the apple cart." "Did you keep me because I was a good worker and could accomplish so much for you? Did you keep me for only what I could do for you?"

She replied, "I realized many years ago that people don't change overnight. I realized that you have to keep waiting and waiting. I always saw the gold in you."

Maybe you cannot be *the* Marlene Evans who travels across this nation speaking in ladies' conferences. Perhaps you cannot be *the* Marlene Evans who edits a ladies' magazine. More than likely you will never author six books. But you **can** be a Marlene Evans who looks for gold. You **can** be a Marlene Evans who keeps waiting for the gold to shine. Let me encourage you that you **can** be a Marlene Evans who is willing to pay any price necessary for the gold to shine in someone and hence, influence another life for eternity!

Let all bitterness,
and wrath, and anger,
and clamour, and evil speaking,
be put away from you,
with all malice:
And be ye kind one to another,
tenderhearted,
forgiving one another,
even as God
for Christ's sake hath forgiven you.
— Ephesians 4:31, 32

CHAPTER SEVEN

GETHSEMANE IS HARDER THAN CALVARY

AFTER TWO MORE weeks of rest that allowed the incision to heal more completely, we returned to Mayo Clinic to begin chemotherapy on May 25, 1994. The following is an article that I wrote for the October 1994 issue of *Christian Womanhood* which describes what basically happened during and after each one of Mrs. Evans' chemotherapy treatments.

Our "Chemo Week," as I call it, begins with Mrs. Evans' and my arriving at 7:00 a.m. at Mayo Clinic on the morning of the treatment. Mrs. Evans has to have her blood drawn to see if it is in good condition for chemotherapy. We then go to the Kahler Coffee Shop and sit at the counter where she orders her favorite breakfast—one soft poached egg, whole wheat toast and a fresh squeezed orange juice. She comments sadly, "I don't want to miss **one** day without my breakfast!" She enjoys the little moments of everything and every day.

After breakfast I push Mrs. Evans in a wheelchair through the underground carpeted halls back to the clinic—a short five to ten minute walk—where Mrs. Evans has a chest x-ray to be sure there is no swelling of the heart, a side effect of one of the drugs she is taking. After that test, we go back to our little apartment so she can rest.

Around 1:00 p.m., we go to the oncology floor to see Dr. Lynn Hartman. The twelfth floor oncology waiting room is always very, very full of all ages and types of people. It is common to see a little ten-year-old girl with no hair—just a baseball cap on—looking very sad as she sits in a wheelchair waiting for her appointment.

Marlene Evans with Dr. Hartman, her oncologist

Mrs. Evans does not like to talk to people there. She likes to read during this time. I recall a Sunday sermon titled, "Gethsemane Is Harder than Calvary," where our preacher describes that waiting for some inevitable "bad" to happen is worse than when the "bad" is actually happening. The reason is because God's grace begins as soon as that hurtful thing happens. Jesus said, "If it be thy will, let this cup pass from Me." God waits to see if we are going to step forward, just as in salvation—He died to save us but we must make the choice to accept. We have a will to choose.

The same principle applies to us when we are facing surgery, a child's divorce, the death of our parents, or any inevitable trauma. We choose how we respond to the hurts God allows to come to our lives. The anticipation of the event produces in most all of us the same feelings Jesus had as He looked ahead to the cross. But, praise God, when we go forward and don't quit, God's marvelous grace is dispensed liberally to cushion the blow as soon as the problem hits.

Now let's go back to Mrs. Evans in the waiting room that is full of cancer patients. She said (and I quote), "My Gethsemane is seeing people in the waiting room on the oncology floor where everyone is locked into a cocoon. They are in an emotional fetal position wanting to do nothing but lick their own wounds. You can only think about surviving the minute. There's no laughing, no crying, no talking, no smiling, no music and no jokes. Every man is an island unto himself—in his own cocoon. When you go into the treatment, it's not as hard as the waiting and watching."

After waiting a half hour, we go in to see Dr. Hartman. After looking over all the reports, she asks Mrs. Evans how she has been doing since her last appointment. Dr. Hartman answers all of our questions. Then we walk to the treatment rooms. There is a choice of a room with a recliner or a room with a bed and a window. Mrs. Evans chooses the room with the window. The *chemotherapy*, meaning *chemical treatment*, is given through an intravenous (I.V.) needle inserted into Mrs. Evans' hand. First she receives a dose of Zofran through the I.V. This is the new anti-emetic drug for control of nausea. Then over a three-hour period, Mrs. Evans receives a "cocktail" of drugs. In this case, she receives three anti-cancer drugs that work on the kind of cancer she has.

She is a remarkable lady. I believe that with the prayers of friends across America and God's help, she can beat this cancer just like she did the first time. The drugs she received are Adriamycin, Cisplatin and 5-FU with the most common side effects being nausea and vomiting, hair loss, fatigue, low blood counts and infections.

At the end of the three hours, Mrs. Evans receives another dose of Zofran. During the three hours, she relaxes and sleeps. It is now about 5:30 p.m. By that time the Clinic is closing for the evening, and the halls begin to empty. Mrs. Evans always wants to go straight to our rented apartment, get in bed and lie still to avoid any movement that could cause a spell of vomiting. Having had chemotherapy previously, Mrs. Evans knows she cannot handle a trip back to Indiana for 48 hours. I then begin giving her two drugs around the clock every three hours—the Zofran pill and Compazine suppositories to prevent the violent sickness she experienced in 1982.

The hardest part of this time period for Mrs. Evans is that she is unable to do anything. In the past when recovering from surgeries, she was able to make phone calls, read, counsel people, etc. However, these drugs make her like a silent robot, which is so unlike Mrs. Evans. She cannot concentrate well enough to read, talk, or do anything. Sometimes she can sleep. Mostly she just lies and stares at the wall. During this chemotherapy treatment, she vomited only three times. She doesn't eat or drink. I try to keep quiet and read or study. Noises bother her because chemo affects the nerves in the brain.

At the end of the second day, Mrs. Evans has a high protein milk shake (Spirulina, Tofu, yogurt or frozen natural yogurt in a fruit or vanilla flavor). We then begin the trip home in stages of how long she can tolerate traveling. The first meal is usually her favorite breakfast on the fourth day after chemo. She has no appetite but does eat the food I fix. I give her a list of foods from which she might like to choose.

I try to spark her interest. The faster she takes in food and fluids, the more rapidly she will regain her strength.

She is very weak for the first seven to nine days, and then begins slowly adding activities. So far, she has been able to start back to church about nine days after each treatment. When she is very weak, she has someone help her apply her makeup and fix her wig. Then someone drives her to church and escorts her in to hear the preaching which she does not want to miss. Her sister and brother-in-law, Doris and Jerry Smith, cared for her beautifully during this time. They took her home from church and made sure she had a Sunday meal before her nap. She takes naps in between church services.

She lost her hair in clumps over a two- to three-week period. Some believe that people will not lose their hair based on their attitude. This is not so. There are many chemotherapy drugs that **do not** cause hair loss. However, Mrs. Evans is taking two drugs that do cause the hair loss. The problem with the hair falling out is that it does so very unevenly.

Mrs. Evans called me one evening and said, "Could you please help me with this hair?" So I got to cut it down to a crew cut for her comfort! We purchased a cute satin headband like babies wear, and one weekend she walked around with her short "do" and a navy headband to match her new navy robe set! She really thought she was cute—and I did too!

Mrs. Evans' course of treatment is one chemotherapy treatment per month every month for six months. Then, she will be x-rayed again to see how the treatment is working. Her first treatment was May 25. Lord willing, she will take her sixth treatment in October. There needs to be a month between treatments because the anti-cancer drugs also affect the white blood count (WBC) which is normally 4,800-10,500. The second week after chemo, Mrs. Evans' WBC goes as low as 1,800. I am amazed she can walk around and attend church, but she does. By the fourth week, the blood rebuilds and is within normal limits again. However, we have been instructed by the doctors that if her WBC falls below 1,000, she should go to the hospital **or** if the WBC stays under 3,000, she is to wait until the WBC count rises before taking chemotherapy again. So far, that hasn't happened to her.

In spite of cancer, Mrs. Evans has a very strong and healthy heart, liver and lungs. She has an outstandingly positive attitude. She continues to enjoy your cards, notes and calls. They are not an intrusion; rather they help her

"Mayo Friends!"

fight this battle. In conclusion, I'd like to leave you with four principles I have seen both my parents and Mrs. Evans use throughout the years of being chronically ill.

1. **Knowledge empowers you!** Read! Read about your disease. When getting books from the library, look for books that are current. I look for books that are practical and easily understood. I peruse the book thoroughly to see if it contains practical things that are within my reach to achieve.

GETHSEMANE IS HARDER THAN CALVARY

Sickness makes everyone feel out of control. The best way to accept a chronic disease is to face it. Make that enemy a friend. Become an expert in that field! You may need to wait until a few weeks after surgery to do this.

Realize there are two approaches to medicine. There is the medical approach and the nutritional approach. Oftentimes, both are needed. Read up on your options. I have used the following for information: Cancer Information Number, 800-4-Cancer; Monday-Friday 7:00 a.m.-5:00 p.m.

I admire Dr. and Mrs. Evans for figuring out a way to get Mrs. Evans to Mayo Clinic where she can receive state-of-the-art medical care for her cancer. On the other hand, she had me do research on which vitamins and nutritional supplements would be good for her to take. Dr. Cal Streeter, a preventive medicine doctor who knows when to use surgeons and traditional medical doctors, has been a great help and support to Mrs. Evans.

Let me give you an example. Mayo Clinic doctors gave Mrs. Evans the drug Cisplatin to kill ovarian cancer cells. One of the side effects is tingling and numbness in the arms and hands. Mrs. Evans was very bothered by this side effect. When we asked our doctor if there was anything we could do about it, she said, "Why don't you work with your local doctor." When we discussed the problem with Dr. Cal Streeter, he advised an injection of B_{12} and folic acid which are vitamins that work on nerve damage. I gave Mrs. Evans this shot and within three to four hours, the annoying sensations were gone. Two shots a week controlled this side effect of chemotherapy. After observing cancer patients for 25 years and caring for Mrs. Evans, I have come to the conclusion that the best way to fight cancer is to take the best of both medical worlds for a combined treatment.

The following is a list of source books that have helped me as I have cared for Mrs. Evans.

Managing the Side Effects of Chemotherapy and Radiation by Marylin J. Dodd, R.N., Ph.D.

The Cancer Dictionary by Roberta Altman and Michael J. Sarg, M.D.

Cancer Therapy: The Independent Consumer's Guide to Non-Toxic Treatment and Prevention by Ralph W. Moss, Ph.D.

Breast Cancer and Ovarian Cancer: Beating the Odds by M. Margaret Kemeny, M.D. and Paula Dranov

When Your Friend Gets Cancer (How You Can Help) by Amy Harwell with Kristine Tomasik

2. **Keep church attendance a priority.** I see so many people do everything the doctor says and quit going to church because they are busy regaining their health. I believe the preaching of God's Word is vital for healing. If you are too weak to take all the steps of getting ready for church, accept help in order to do so.

3. **Remember, *"A merry heart doeth good like a medicine. "*** A merry heart is curative! After you face the facts and have started a regimen of treatment, forget yourself and enjoy life! Don't miss the sunsets, a meal at Cracker Barrel Restaurant, a drive to the lake, and so on as Mrs. Evans does. Mrs. Evans and I have times of "Laugh Therapy." Sometimes

we tell funny stories that have happened to us, and we are guaranteed some good belly laughs which I call internal jogging! It's good for the organs!

Other times we talk to people who make us laugh like Leslie Beaman from Toledo, Ohio, or Pastor and Mrs. Sheldon Schearer from Great Falls, Montana.

4. **Continue to live for others.** If often amazes me when I see Mrs. Evans being so careful of people's feelings. She is taking care of herself. She is eating healthy and taking vitamins and supplements. Yet, she is not too consumed about her health to reach out to others.

5. **Look at the lighter side of life in the midst of your battles.** Much discussion had gone on between Dr. Evans, Mrs. Evans and me regarding the price of the anti-nausea drug, Zofran. The football-shaped pills are $17.25 for each pill. Mayo Clinic sent us home after each treatment with 15 pills—for a total cost of $258.50.

Every three hours I would wake Mrs. Evans to give her medication. This would go on for several days. To break the monotony of the routine I began saying, "It's time to take your $17 'football.' " Sometimes, before the three-hour time lapse was completed, she would raise her eyebrows and ask, "Is it time for me to take a 'football' yet?"

One night after giving her the Zofran, she immediately vomited the pill. I said, "Well, there goes that $20 'football' down the drain."

She answered dryly with a quirk, "Does the price of the 'football' rise when it comes back up?!"

The full impact of her humor did not really sink in to me until Dr. Evans said a few days later, "Hey, Carol, I heard about the price increase on those 'footballs' when Marlene brings them back up!" We have laughed many times since, and Mrs. Evans has told the story to close friends, like our dentist of two decades, Dr. Robert Thornton who has a great sense of humor. One day while I sat in the dental chair, he was asking me about Mrs. Evans' condition. Dr. Thornton commented, "Carol, I heard about those $20 'footballs'!!"

Thank God for new drugs which are made available, such as Zofran, which allowed Mrs. Evans to go through chemo-therapy with little vomiting and enabled her to retain her great sense of humor.

6. **When facing a serious battle for the second time, realize you are a veteran and that you have strength to triumph.** Dr. Hartman told Mrs. Evans, "You are a veteran. You know more about chemotherapy than we doctors do." As we discussed facing the second regimen of chemotherapy, I asked Mrs. Evans, "How can you do this when you know what chemo does to you?"

Her answer..."I want to live!"

CHAPTER EIGHT

CONVALESCENCE

W E SPENT THE summer returning to Mayo Clinic every month for chemotherapy treatments, recuperating and also traveling to all of Mrs. Evans' speaking engagements. Other than cancelling two meetings, Mrs. Evans was able to travel to all of her other engagements.

No activity is ever normal when Mrs. Evans is involved! For example, she has her "ways" to keep any trip from being mundane and boring! She plans her stops around restaurants and scenery. This means that sometimes we eat salad at one restaurant, our main meal at another restaurant, and dessert at a third restaurant. Some of her favorite eating places are the Machine Shed in Rockford, Illinois, which is completely decorated with farm machinery and tools, the Cracker Barrel in Madison, Wisconsin, and Burnstadt's European Café in Tomah, Wisconsin, where we stop for homemade rhubarb pie.

During these trips, we have many great conversations. It seems that on every little excursion we take, Mrs. Evans says something that I feel I need to record. Mostly the statements she makes have to do with how to have more eternal influence, how to win souls, and how to treat people with love and kindness. The following is an example of something she taught me on one of our trips.

"Often older people do not feel their clothes are very important. But the sad fact is, younger people will treat older people according to how they are dressed. Of course, this is superficial and worldly thinking, but it is realistic thinking. When the older person is dressed stylishly, minimizing her figure flaws, and enhancing her face, it draws the younger person to find the soul, the spirit, the personality, the wisdom and the experience of the older person. Since the older are to teach the younger as Titus 2 instructs, it is not a matter of our wants regarding clothes, but of our being able to leave our works on earth in order to have our rewards in Heaven."

One of the highlights of Mrs. Evans' summer was spending time on the tri-level outdoor deck that had been added to the back of her home. The deck was designed and built expressly for Mrs. Evans by Brother Forrest Depper and Brother Roy Moffitt. Relatives along with well over 100 dear friends from First Baptist Church of Hammond, staff and faculty members of Hyles-Anderson College and friends from churches all over America donated the money for the deck. A friend in First Baptist Church of Hammond, Mrs. Pat Phares, provided a beautiful patio set for one level of the deck. A beautiful glider Mrs. Evans had admired was anonymously given to her, which she used for many hours swinging with her grandchildren.

Another summer highlight was a private fireworks display orchestrated by Dave Christensen and Dan Mock with Mr. and Mrs. Mock to supervise. It was a 45-minute, non-stop show for Mrs. Evans and family members to enjoy. At the end, with sparkler in hand, Mrs. Evans was very euphoric.

She said, "Just think, those college-age boys thought enough of me to take their time and put on that show!"

Jeff and Joy Ryder felt they should return home from the jungles of Papua New Guinea to be with Mrs. Evans. They arrived on July 18 to a "Christmas in July" party decorated and provided by their friends and supporters, Eric and Tammy Sapp. The gifts included clothing and shoes not worn in the jungle which the Ryders would need in the months to come.

A missionary apartment provided by First Baptist Church of Hammond was completely redecorated with the help of many individuals, families and groups from the church supervised by Belinda Casteel and June Ryland. Mrs. Evans has mentioned more than once, "There is no way I could have helped Jeff and Joy re-enter America." By this time she was halfway through the six-month chemotherapy regimen and was experiencing the side effects that go with it.

With each treatment, there is a build-up of toxicity in the body which causes the patient to lose weight and experience extreme fatigue with these symptoms becoming increasingly worse. Therefore, Mrs. Evans became increasingly fatigued and withdrawn.

Mrs. Evans and her daughter, Joy

On our Mayo Clinic trip for July, Mrs. Evans, Joy and I traveled to Minnesota together. Joy and I had a wonderful time talking and shopping while Mrs. Evans slept off the effects of chemotherapy. This became an important time for Joy to begin accepting what was happening in her mother's life. Joy wanted to learn about everything medical I was doing for her mother. Joy and her mom discussed at length the fact that Joy and her family needed to go back to the mission field. Mrs. Evans had been adamant that Joy follow Jeff and allow Jeff to follow his calling to the foreign mission field. I remember one time Joy's saying, "Mom, do you realize I have to accept the fact that the rest of the world gets to take care of you while I'm off in PNG?"

On the trip home from Mayo Clinic, I chose to listen to Dr. Hyles' tape, "May I Please Change Seats." Mrs. Evans was sleeping in the front seat, groggy from chemotherapy. Joy was in the back seat, crying. I was driving and hoping that everything Dr. Hyles had said about Mrs. Evans on the tape would be a blessing to Joy. That trip home was a decisive time for Joy where she accepted the "seat" in which she has to sit. Joy has been wonderful to me and expressed her gratitude to me in regards to the care I give to her mother. I don't know if I were in Joy's seat if I could do the same.

I admire Joy so much because she had to have so many—what I call—"acceptance ceremonies" while she was home on furlough. Another turning point in Joy's life was the following conversation she had with her dad.

They discussed at length what would happen should Mrs. Evans go to Heaven during Joy's next term on the mission field. It helps Joy to talk out all the possibilities and ramifications. While discussing what could happen to Dr.

Evans if Mrs. Evans was out of his life, he said to her, "I doubt if I would ever marry again if your mother goes to Heaven because no woman will ever accept me totally the way your mother does."

School Begins!

With the fall coming, a different set of problems reared their ugly heads. Mrs. Evans was too weak to get ready for school, but she did not want to lie home in bed all day. She was very scared about missing school and not fulfilling her responsibilities. We made arrangements that I would go over early in the morning to help get her ready and drive her to school.

One day she was so helpless and depressed that I said, "You should stay home."

She said, "I will not think good if I lie in bed. If you can get me to school, and I can teach my classes, then I will come home and my bed will feel good."

Even though I thought she should stay home, I obeyed her wishes. This included fixing her a breakfast which she did not want to eat. However, I always say Mrs. Evans is the easiest patient in the world for whom to care because she follows instructions implicitly. She ate without appetite in order to have strength to teach her classes. As the chemotherapy treatments progressed, Mrs. Evans continually became weaker. Eventually, in order to teach her classes, she used a wheelchair—enabling her to keep teaching Biblical philosophies. Mrs. Evans is a very "mobile" teacher, so she sacrificed her preference and remained seated in the chair while teaching in order to **keep** teaching.

Not only was she faithful to school, she remained faithful to her church. Several of her workers delivered her right to the front doors of the church. Sometimes, it was just in time for the preaching. We would walk her in, escort her right to her seat, pick her up and take her right out because she was too weak to talk with people. She told me repeatedly, "I have to hear Dr. Hyles' preaching. He is getting me through this chemotherapy. I couldn't face life if it weren't for his preaching."

In spite of damaging drugs pouring into her veins, Mrs. Evans' priorities were still intact. Family, church and school were in the forefront of her mind at all times. She rarely missed. She stopped eating out at restaurants to save herself for church. She stopped almost all social engagements.

I would like to share some thoughts about how to live with a terminal illness.

1. **Talk about the sickness.** If your sickness is cancer, call it cancer. You don't make life normal again by trying to hide what is wrong.

2. **Accept death as a part of life.** It is.

3. **Consider each day another day of life.** It is a wonderful gift from God to be enjoyed as fully as possible.

4. **Realize life is never going to be perfect.** It wasn't before, and it won't be now.

5. **Pray.** Prayer is your strength. Philippians 4:6, 7 says, *"Be careful for nothing; but in every thing by prayer and*

supplication with thanksgiving let your requests be made known unto God. And the peace of God, which passeth all understanding, shall keep your hearts and minds through Christ Jesus."

6. **Learn to live *with* your illness instead of considering yourself dying *from* it.** In reality, every person who lives is, in essence, dying in some way.

7. **Put your friends and relatives at ease.** Be honest and forthright about what is happening in your life. If you don't want pity, don't ask for it.

8. **Take time to make all arrangements for funerals, wills, etc.** Choose your favorite songs. It is not a bad idea to purchase your cemetery lot and headstone. Doing all of this in advance simplifies the Homegoing of the loved one for the family. Make certain your family knows and understands all these arrangements.

9. **Set new goals by taking into consideration your new limitations.** The simple things of life become most enjoyable.

10. **Talk with family as new problems arise.** Include the children in these conversations as much as possible. Remember your problem is not an individual one.

CHAPTER NINE

"WHY, GOD?"

I KNOW MANY OF you reading this book could join me in admitting that you would like to ask God, "Why does it have to be Mrs. Evans again?" Or possibly you are asking that very question about yourself or someone you love.

When I am tempted to ask this question, I realize I must turn to the only place I can find a satisfying answer—the eternal Word of God. I **know** that something good has to come out of Mrs. Evans' diagnosis of ovarian cancer as I read and must rest on Romans 8:28 which says, *"And we know that all things work together for good to them that love God, to them who are the called according to his purpose."* However, when the news of her ovarian cancer came to me, this one verse did not seem to answer all of my questions and calm all of my fears.

When I am faced with a difficult situation in life, I keep reading my Bible until I receive peace. This time, rather than allow myself to question God or become bitter, I decided to do a Bible study on suffering. In so doing, I found that God has many reasons for allowing us to suffer.

I am including part of the Bible study that helped me to

see God's purpose in suffering, and also gave me the peace I so needed. I trust as you read and meditate on these verses in your Bible study time that they will be just the "dose of Scripture" you need for whatever problems you are facing in your life.

➢ **God allows suffering to produce the fruit of patience**. *"And not only so, but we glory in tribulations also: knowing that tribulation worketh patience."* (Romans 5:3)

"Knowing this, that the trying of your faith worketh patience. But let patience have her perfect work, that ye may be perfect and entire, wanting nothing." (James 1:3-4)

➢ **God allows suffering to produce the fruit of joy**. *"For his anger endureth but a moment; in his favour is life: weeping may endure for a night, but joy cometh in the morning."* (Psalm 30:5)

"They that sow in tears shall reap in joy. He that goeth forth and weepeth, bearing precious seed, shall doubtless come again with rejoicing, bringing his sheaves with him." (Psalms 126:5-6)

➢ **God allows suffering to produce the fruit of maturity**. *"It is better to go to the house of mourning, than to go to the house of feasting: for that is the end of all men; and the living will lay it to his heart. Sorrow is better than laughter: for by the sadness of the countenance the heart is made better. The heart of the wise is in the house of mourning; but the heart of fools is in the house of mirth."* (Ecclesiastes 7:2-4)

➢ **God allows suffering to produce the fruit of**

righteousness. *"Now no chastening for the present seemeth to be joyous, but grievous: nevertheless afterward it yieldeth the peaceable fruit of righteousness unto them which are exercised thereby."* (Hebrews 12:11)

➤ **God allows suffering in order to silence the devil**. *"And the LORD said unto Satan, Hast thou considered my servant Job, that there is none like him in the earth, a perfect and an upright man, one that feareth God, and escheweth evil? Then Satan answered the LORD, and said, Doth Job fear God for nought? Hast not thou made an hedge about him, and about his house, and about all that he hath on every side? thou hast blessed the work of his hands, and his substance is increased in the land...Then Job arose, and rent his mantle, and shaved his head, and fell down upon the ground, and worshiped, And said, Naked came I out of my mother's womb, and naked shall I return thither: the LORD gave, and the LORD hath taken away; blessed be the name of the LORD. In all this Job sinned not, nor charged God foolishly."* (Job 1:8-10; 20-22)

➤ **God allows suffering to teach us**. *"Before I was afflicted I went astray: but now have I kept thy word...It is good for me that I have been afflicted; that I might learn thy statues."* (Psalms 119:67, 71)

➤ **God allows suffering to purify our lives**. *"But he knoweth the way that I take: when he hath tried me, I shall come forth as gold."* (Job 23:10)

"For thou, O God, hast proved us: thou hast tried us, as silver is tried. Thou broughtest us into the net; thou laidst affliction upon our loins. Thou hast caused men to ride over our heads; we went through fire and through water: but thou

broughtest us out into a wealthy place. " (Psalms 66:10-12)

"And I will turn my hand upon thee, and purely purge away thy dross, and take away all thy tin. " (Isaiah 1:25)

"Behold, I have refined thee, but not with silver; I have chosen thee in the furnace of affliction. " (Isaiah 48:10)

"The fining pot is for silver, and the furnace for gold: but the Lord trieth the hearts. " (Proverbs 17:3)

"That the trial of your faith, being much more precious than of gold that perisheth, though it be tried with fire, might be found unto praise and honour and glory at the appearing of Jesus Christ. " (I Peter 1:7)

➤ **God allows suffering to help us become like Christ.** *"Beloved, think it not strange concerning the fiery trial which is to try you, as though some strange thing happened unto you: But rejoice, inasmuch as ye are partakers of Christ's sufferings; that, when his glory shall be revealed, ye may be glad also with exceeding joy.* " (I Peter 4:12, 13)

"Furthermore we have had fathers of our flesh which corrected us, and we gave them reverence: shall we not much rather be in subjection unto the Father of spirits, and live? For they verily for a few days chastened us after their own pleasure; but he for our profit, that we might be partakers of his holiness. " (Hebrews 12:9, 10)

"That I may know him, and the power of his resurrection, and the fellowship of his sufferings, being made conformable unto his death. " (Philippians 3:10)

"WHY, GOD?"

"But we have this treasure in earthen vessels, that the excellency of the power may be of God, and not of us. We are troubled on every side, yet not distressed; we are perplexed, but not in despair; Persecuted, but not forsaken; cast down, but not destroyed; Always bearing about in the body the dying of the Lord Jesus, that the life also of Jesus might be made manifest in our body. " (II Corinthians 4:7-10)

➤ **God allows suffering to bring glory to Himself.**
"And call upon me in the day of trouble: I will deliver thee, and thou shalt glorify me. " (Psalm 50:15)

"And as Jesus passed by, he saw a man which was blind from his birth. And his disciples asked him, saying, Master, who did sin, this man, or his parents, that he was born blind? Jesus answered, Neither hath this man sinned, nor his parents: but that the works of God should be made manifest in him. " (John 9:1-3)

"Now a certain man was sick, named Lazarus, of Bethany, the town of Mary and her sister Martha. (It was that Mary which anointed the Lord with ointment, and wiped his feet with her hair, whose brother Lazarus was sick.) Therefore his sisters sent unto him, saying, Lord, behold, he whom thou lovest is sick. When Jesus heard that, he said, This sickness is not unto death, but for the glory of God, that the Son of God might be glorified thereby. " (John 11:1-4)

"Verily, verily, I say unto thee, When thou wast young, thou girdedst thyself, and walkedst whither thou wouldest: but when thou shalt be old, thou shalt stretch forth thy hands, and another shall gird thee, and carry thee whither thou wouldest not. This spake he, signifying by what death he should glorify God. And when he had spoken this, he saith

unto him, Follow me." (John 21:18, 19)

"For I know that this shall turn to my salvation through your prayer, and the supply of the Spirit of Jesus Christ, According to my earnest expectation and my hope, that in nothing I shall be ashamed, but that with all boldness, as always, so now also Christ shall be magnified in my body, whether it be by life, or by death." (Philippians 1:19, 20)

➤ **God allows suffering to keep us from sinning.** *"And lest I should be exalted above measure through the abundance of the revelations, there was given to me a thorn in the flesh, the messenger of Satan to buffet me, lest I should be exalted above measure."* (II Corinthians 12:7)

"And he said unto me, My grace is sufficient for thee: for my strength is made perfect in weakness. Most gladly therefore will I rather glory in my infirmities, that the power of Christ may rest upon me. Therefore I take pleasure in infirmities, in reproaches, in necessities, in persecutions, in distresses for Christ's sake: for when I am weak, then am I strong." (II Corinthians 12:9, 10)

➤ **God allows suffering to make us confess when we do sin.** *"I acknowledged my sin unto thee, and mine iniquity have I not hid. I said, I will confess my transgressions unto the Lord; and thou forgavest the iniquity of my sin. Selah."* (Psalm 32:5)

"And the children of Israel did evil again in the sight of the Lord, and served Baalim, and Ashtaroth, and the gods of Syria, and the gods of Zidon, and the gods of Moab, and the gods of the children of Ammon, and the gods of the Philistines, and forsook the Lord, and served not him. And the

anger of the LORD was hot against Israel, and he sold them into the hands of the Philistines, and into the hands of the children of Ammon." (Judges 10:6, 7)

"And the children of Israel said unto the LORD, We have sinned: do thou unto us whatsoever seemeth good unto thee; deliver us only, we pray thee, this day. And they put away the strange gods from among them, and served the LORD: and his soul was grieved for the misery of Israel." (Judges 10:15, 16)

"Now for a long season Israel hath been without the true God, and without a teaching priest, and without law. But when they in their trouble did turn unto the LORD God of Israel, and sought him, he was found of them." (II Chronicles 15:3, 4)

"I will go and return to my place, till they acknowledge their offence, and seek my face: in their affliction they will seek me early." (Hosea 5:15)

➤ **God allows suffering to prove our sonship.** *"And ye have forgotten the exhortation which speaketh unto you as unto children, My son, despise not thou the chastening of the Lord, nor faint when thou art rebuked of him: For whom the Lord loveth he chasteneth, and scourgeth every son whom he receiveth."* (Hebrews 12:5, 6)

➤ **God allows suffering to chasten us for our sin.** *"Furthermore we have had fathers of our flesh which corrected us, and we gave them reverence: shall we not much rather be in subjection unto the Father of spirits, and live? For they verily for a few days chastened us after their own pleasure; but he for our profit, that we might be partakers of* *his holiness.*" (Hebrews 12:9, 10)

➢ **God allows suffering to reveal ourselves to ourselves, that we may see ourselves for what we really are.** *"Wherefore I abhor myself, and repent in dust and ashes."* (Job 42:6)

"I will arise and go to my father, and will say unto him, Father, I have sinned against heaven, and before thee." (Luke 15:18)

➢ **God allows suffering to help strengthen our prayer life.** *"LORD, in trouble have they visited thee, they poured out a prayer when thy chastening was upon them."* (Isaiah 26:16)

➢ **God allows suffering to allow us to become an example to others.** *"But in all things approving ourselves as the ministers of God, in much patience, in afflictions, in necessities, in distresses, In stripes, in imprisonments, in tumults, in labours, in watchings, in fastings."* (II Corinthians 6:4, 5)

"And ye became followers of us, and of the Lord, having received the word in much affliction, with joy of the Holy Ghost: So that ye were ensamples to all that believe in Macedonia and Achaia." (I Thessalonians 1:6, 7)

➢ **God allows suffering to help qualify us as counselors.** *"Rejoice with them that do rejoice, and weep with them that weep."* (Romans 12:15)

"Bear ye one another's burdens, and so fulfil the law of Christ." (Galatians 6:2)

"WHY, GOD?"

"Blessed be God, even the Father of our Lord Jesus Christ, the Father of mercies, and the God of all comfort; Who comforteth us in all our tribulation, that we may be able to comfort them which are in any trouble, by the comfort wherewith we ourselves are comforted of God. For as the sufferings of Christ abound in us, so our consolation also aboundeth by Christ." (II Corinthians 1:3-5)

➤ **God allows suffering to further the Gospel witness.** *"But I would ye should understand, brethren, that the things which happened unto me have fallen out rather unto the furtherance of the gospel; So that my bonds in Christ are manifest in all the palace, and in all other places."* (Philippians 1:12, 13)

"And Saul was consenting unto his death. And at that time there was a great persecution against the church which was at Jerusalem; and they were all scattered abroad throughout the regions of Judæa and Samaria, except the apostles. And devout men carried Stephen to his burial, and made great lamentation over him. As for Saul, he made havock of the church, entering into every house, and haling men and women committed them to prison. Therefore they that were scattered abroad went every where preaching the word." (Acts 8:1-4)

"For I am now ready to be offered, and the time of my departure is at hand. I have fought a good fight, I have finished my course, I have kept the faith: Henceforth there is laid up for me a crown of righteousness, which the Lord, the righteous judge, shall give me at that day: and not to me only, but unto all them also that love his appearing." (II Timothy 4:6-8)

"At my first answer no man stood with me, but all men

99

forsook me: I pray God that it may not be laid to their charge. Notwithstanding the Lord stood with me, and strengthened me; that by me the preaching might be fully known, and that all the Gentiles might hear: and I was delivered out of the mouth of the lion. " (II Timothy 4:16, 17)

Also, please read Acts 16:25-34.

➢ **God allows suffering to make us more than conquerors**. *"Who shall separate us from the love of Christ? shall tribulation, or distress, or persecution, or famine, or nakedness, or peril, or sword?...Nay, in all these things we are more than conquerors through him that loved us."* (Romans 8:35, 37)

"Now thanks be unto God, which always causeth us to triumph in Christ, and maketh manifest the savour of his knowledge by us in every place." (II Corinthians 2:14)

➢ **God allows suffering to give us insight into God's nature**. *"I have heard of thee by the hearing of the ear: but now mine eye seeth thee."* (Job 42:5)

"For as many as are led by the Spirit of God, they are the sons of God. For ye have not received the spirit of bondage again to fear; but ye have received the Spirit of adoption, whereby we cry, Abba, Father." (Romans 8:14, 15)

"For I reckon that the sufferings of this present time are not worthy to be compared with the glory which shall be revealed in us." (Romans 8:18)

➢ **God allows suffering to drive us closer to God**. *"If ye be reproached for the name of Christ, happy are ye; for the* *spirit of glory and of God resteth upon you: on their part he is evil spoken of, but on your part he is glorified."* (I Peter 4:14)

"Therefore I take pleasure in infirmities, in reproaches, in necessities, in persecutions, in distresses for Christ's sake: for when I am weak, then am I strong." (II Corinthians 12:10)

➤ **God allows suffering to prepare us for a greater ministry.** *"Verily, verily, I say unto you, Except a corn of wheat fall into the ground and die, it abideth alone: but if it die, it bringeth forth much fruit."* (John 12:24)

Also, please read I Kings 17 and I Kings 18.

➤ **God allows suffering to provide for us a reward.** *"Blessed are they which are persecuted for righteousness' sake: for theirs is the kingdom of heaven. Blessed are ye, when men shall revile you, and persecute you, and shall say all manner of evil against you falsely, for my sake. Rejoice, and be exceeding glad: for great is your reward in heaven: for so persecuted they the prophets which were before you."* (Matthew 5:10-12)

"Then answered Peter and said unto him, Behold, we have forsaken all, and followed thee; what shall we have therefore? And Jesus said unto them, Verily I say unto you, That ye which have followed me, in the regeneration when the Son of man shall sit in the throne of his glory, ye also shall sit upon twelve thrones, judging the twelve tribes of Israel. And every one that hath forsaken houses, or brethren, or sisters, or father, or mother, or wife, or children, or lands, for my name's sake, shall receive an hundredfold, and shall inherit

everlasting life. " (Matthew 19:27-29)

"The Spirit itself beareth witness with our spirit, that we are the children of God: and if children, then heirs; heirs of God, and joint-heirs with Christ; if so be that we suffer with him, that we may be also glorified together." (Romans 8:16, 17)

"For our light affliction, which is but for a moment, worketh for us a far more exceeding and eternal weight of glory." (II Corinthians 4:17)

➢ **God allows suffering to prepare us for the kingdom.** *"Which is a manifest token of the righteous judgment of God, that ye may be counted worthy of the kingdom of God, for which ye also suffer."* (II Thessalonians 1:5)

"If we suffer, we shall also reign with him: if we deny him, he also will deny us." (II Timothy 2:12)

➢ **God allows suffering to show God's sovereignty.** *"And we know that all things work together for good to them that love God, to them who are the called according to his purpose."* (Romans 8:28)

"There hath no temptation taken you but such as is common to man: but God is faithful, who will not suffer you to be tempted above that ye are able; but will with the temptation also make a way to escape, that ye may be able to bear it." (I Corinthians 10:13)

"For thou, O God, hast proved us: thou hast tried us, as silver is tried. Thou broughtest us into the net; thou laidst

affliction upon our loins. Thou hast caused men to ride over our heads; we went through fire and through water: but thou broughtest us out into a wealthy place. " (Psalms 66:10-12)

"*But as for you, ye thought evil against me; but God meant it unto good, to bring to pass, as it is this day, to save much people alive.* " (Genesis 50:20)

"*Now therefore be not grieved, nor angry with yourselves, that ye sold me hither: for God did send me before you to preserve life. For these two years hath the famine been in the land: and yet there are five years, in the which there shall neither be earing nor harvest. And God sent me before you to preserve you a posterity in the earth, and to save your lives by a great deliverance. So now it was not you that sent me hither, but God: and he hath made me a father to Pharaoh, and lord of all his house, and a ruler throughout all the land of Egypt.* " (Genesis 45:5-8)

PART II

by
Marlene Evans

CHAPTER TEN

"WHAT TO DO WHEN THE DOCTOR SAYS, "IT'S CANCER!"

W HAT ARE YOU going to do if or when the doctor says, "It's cancer!"? I am sure no one wants to hear those words, and yet, statistics show that one out of every four people will hear these devastating words sometime in her lifetime unless the cure that is being promised is found very soon.

Two Christian physicians in our area, Dr. Cal Streeter, a doctor with a preventative health specialty who has written articles on health for *Christian Womanhood*, and his brother, Dr. Dennis Streeter, a well-known surgeon, both say they believe that the food we put into our bodies has much to do with the high rate of cancer in our country. We are also seeing a great deal of written material, especially in the periodicals, about food and its relationship to cancer.

Those who are fortunate enough not to have to hear the words, "It's cancer," in their lifetime will probably be talking with friends who have the disease or with family members who have been told, "It's cancer."

I recall that my mother and dad had cancer; a grandma had cancer, a grandpa had cancer, three or four uncles had cancer, and three or four aunts all had cancer. Both sides of my family seem to have been riddled with it, which seems to be true of many families.

Stop and count how many in your family or in your church have been told, "It's cancer." Possibly cancer is not the big hurt you or those you love face. No matter what the heartache, this chapter will be useful in helping those around you or in helping you, even though most of us like to think we will never be told that we have cancer.

Great Gulps of Scripture

I believe that the first step to take when the doctor says, "It's cancer!" is to run to Jesus and to the Bible for great gulps of Scripture. Don't panic or go into hysterics. Don't yell and scream. Don't walk—**run** to Jesus. You can stave off fear this way.

On August 6, 1982, I was told "It's cancer!" I went in to have surgery to remove a lump in the breast and woke up to be told I had had a mastectomy. I know from experience that you can fight off the fear by going directly to the Scriptures. Some people have said in referring to me and the way I have responded to the diagnosis of cancer that I am a remarkable woman. I am not remarkable; I do have a remarkable God Who has given me a remarkable Book to help not just me, but **every** Christian respond in a remarkable way!

Getting into the Bible will also increase a person's prospects of recovering if the cancer is not terminal. Even if your cancer is terminal, trusting in the Lord while you live may cause you to live longer and will certainly give you a better quality of life while you do live. You will always feel better, no matter what the ultimate outcome, if you can face the problem with a relaxed, calm spirit and a good dose of Scripture to sustain you.

Of course, I am taking for granted that I am writing to those who have accepted Jesus Christ as their Saviour and had a time in their lives when they asked Him to save them from sin and take them to Heaven when they die. You are going to go to Heaven when you die if you are a Christian—if you have asked Christ's pardon for your sin and know Christ as your personal Saviour. His blood has cleansed your sin.

A person who is full of anxiety and fear will bring nothing except more suffering on herself, on those she loves, and on those who are caring for her. You may say, "But I'm just the type that wrings my hands. I fret a lot. I'm a worrier and there is nothing I can do about it."

If you would describe yourself in this way and have never been told you have cancer, but already know that this would be your pattern of behavior, read this very carefully because you are going to need to get ready. Whether it will be cancer or something in your family which will shock and hurt you as much as cancer would, you are going to want to be ready for whatever God allows in your life.

Psalm 119:165 says, *"Great peace have they which love thy law, and nothing shall offend them."* That word *offend* covers being upset. You can be told, "It's cancer!" and not be upset. Now, please don't misunderstand. You will not jump up and down and clap your hands with glee. No one wants to have cancer. However, according to this verse, God gives us the opportunity to have peace through the storm.

If you are told, "It is cancer," you do not have to be devastated about your diagnosis if you are in the Word of God. *"Great peace have they which love thy law* (love the Word of God), *and nothing* (not even a diagnosis of cancer) *shall offend them. "* In direct proportion to how much you are in the Word of God and to how much you have a love relationship—rather than a flirtation—with the Word of God is how much you will or will not be upset when you are told, "It's cancer."

There are so many wonderful verses that there is no way I could give them all to you. If you are searching for Scriptures, think on Isaiah 40:29-31 which says, *"He giveth power to the faint, and to them that have no might He increaseth strength. Even the youths shall faint and be weary, and the young men shall utterly fall, but they that wait upon the LORD shall renew their strength; they shall mount up with wings as eagles. They shall run and not be weary, and they shall walk and not faint. "*

My husband was telling me the other day about listening to the Psalms on tape in his car. He said that after listening to four or five Psalms, he had such peace in his mind and soul. And you can have that same peace, no matter what bad news comes your way. Whatever negative report comes about you, your husband, your mother, your father, an uncle, an aunt or a child can be taken peacefully if you dwell on Scripture. Dwell on Scriptures like Isaiah 40:29-31.

I have written the word "cancer" next to Isaiah 41:10a in my Bible which says, *"Fear thou not; for I am with thee: Be not dismayed; for I am thy God. "* I do not have to be discouraged. I don't have to live in despair, nor do I have to be perplexed, bewildered and walk around saying, "Why me?"

Why *Not* Me?

Why *not* me? When good things happen to me, I surely don't question God's wisdom by saying, "Why me?" Then why should I question His wisdom when He allows a seeming tragedy to come into my life? (Incidentally, I am not even sure that cancer is bad for me. God allowed it to happen in my life, and I have always believed that what He allows can only be for my good and His glory.)

Isaiah 41:10 concludes by saying, *"I will strengthen thee; yea, I will help thee; yea, I will uphold thee with the right hand of my righteousness."* What a great promise! He will help me through the trial of cancer. He has promised to hold me up with His hand!

Think a while about Romans 12:1, 2 which says, *"I beseech you therefore, brethren, by the mercies of God, that ye present your bodies a living sacrifice, holy, acceptable unto God, which is your reasonable service. And be not conformed to this world: but be ye transformed by the renewing of your mind, that ye may prove what is that good, and acceptable, and perfect, will of God."* These are such familiar Scriptures, and yet we live as if we don't know of their existence.

When heartache comes, people will sometimes make statements like, "God is punishing me," or "God is unfair," or "God hates me." Rather than thinking these natural thoughts, why not take the suffering as God wanting to teach you or help you become a better person. So, don't succumb to wrong thinking. Be *"transformed by the renewing of your mind."* Ask yourself questions such as, "What good could I get out of this?" "What good can come from having cancer?" "What verses do I know to help me through this?" To be sure, the world looks at disease, heartache and problems in a different way than what Christians should. Yes, I need to ask myself, "Why **not** me?"

You Can Face, "It's Cancer!"

One of the finest ladies I know is a tremendous wife, mother, Christian and soul winner. As you converse with her, it is obvious that she possesses a God-given depth of wisdom and grace.

While still a teenager, she was diagnosed with Multiple Sclerosis, a crippling disease which is almost harder to understand than cancer. Though the medical field continues to study the ravages of MS, very little is known about how or why the disease strikes an individual. In fact, the very medicines used in the treatment of Multiple Sclerosis often cause more degeneration than healing. Quite simply, very little can be done for someone who has the disease of Multiple Sclerosis.

Recently I heard that this pastor's wife was diagnosed with cancer and was undergoing treatment. I was concerned so I called her. Her attitude was unbelievable. It was not a shallow, sickening sweet, "Oh, everything's just all right." Rather, her statements showed depth and sincerity such as, "Some blessings have already come from this added disease. The Lord has really shown Himself to us, and He has already done some great things for us."

WHEN THE DOCTOR SAYS, "IT'S CANCER!"

I thought to myself, "This is so far from how the world responds!" You see, the Scripture can cause a renewing of our minds, and that is exactly what we need. We need it for when the doctor says, "It's cancer!" as well as for every other heartache that life brings. We need something totally opposite of what the world is capable of showing us!

Run to Jesus, and run to the Word of God so that you can face, "It's cancer!" or any other heartache. You will be able to confront your difficulty with the confidence that God has allowed it for your good and His glory. I can promise you that He will go through this valley with you!

CHAPTER ELEVEN

YOU'RE A WHOLE WOMAN!

IN THE LAST few years, the world has gone wild producing true-to-life stories in every possible format to combat the feelings of inadequacy women suffer with a mastectomy. At some time during the account, a woman is usually featured sitting in front of a mirror staring at her scar with tears rolling down her cheeks. Our world today has gone crazy over the importance of the physical appearance of the body.

One can hardly drive down any major highway without seeing billboards that promote every kind of enhancement for the physical body. One can hardly enter any shopping mall without the same type of sensual bombardment. The suggestiveness is absolutely everywhere, including in today's newspapers, magazines, catalogs, and even on the envelopes from credit card companies in which we are to mail our payments.

With all of this emphasis on the physical body, it is not difficult to understand why losing a body part such as a breast would be such a devastating experience for women who have not emphasized the complete person, including the body, the soul and the spirit. *"And the very God of peace sanctify you*

*wholly; and I pray God your whole spirit and soul and body
be preserved blameless unto the coming of our Lord Jesus
Christ."* (I Thessalonians 5:23)

Christian women who have had mastectomies have said to
me that they no longer feel like a whole woman. How could
that be? The woman who has had a mastectomy still has a
body which allows her to walk, do her work, love and live.
We still have our spirits, minds and souls. It is not what's on
a woman's body which makes her loved, respected and
desired, but it is that which is in her heart and the way in
which she relates to others.

If you are having these types of feelings, realize that, of
course, you are a whole woman; you can still be every bit the
woman that God wants you to be.

Forsake the world's thinking and emphasis on the physical
body, and concentrate on developing your soul and spirit.
*"That the righteousness of the law might be fulfilled in us,
who walk not after the flesh, but after the Spirit. For they that
are after the flesh do mind the things of the flesh; but they that
are after the Spirit the things of the Spirit."* (Romans 8:4, 5)

CHAPTER TWELVE

CHEMOTHERAPY: THROUGH SHADES OF HELL!

I HAVE TRIED to remember the myriad of feelings I experienced while going through my first episode of chemotherapy without Zofran, a drug which helps control the side effects of chemotherapy. Of course, my second regimen of chemo was much easier. I had just a few days after each treatment where I felt I "missed life;" I didn't want noise, people, food, schedule or light. In fact, some people now take their treatment and immediately return to work. I know a 44-year-old teacher of whom this is true. *Let me emphasize again that the side effects were **not** nearly as extreme in 1994.*

Chemotherapy took a tremendous toll on my emotions for months after my 1982 treatments. Interestingly enough, I have had people with chronic illnesses such as lupus, rheumatoid arthritis, diabetes, fibromyalgia, infectious mononucleosis, and so forth tell me they have had to fight the same feelings or characteristics at different times that I battled.

For example, I could not concentrate well enough to talk to my husband, but neither did I want him to read the paper when we went out for breakfast. I felt alone, but I did not

want people. I felt angry that people thought I could work but
didn't want them to take over my jobs either. Following are
some of my feelings and characteristics after chemotherapy:

doubted the reality of God	*claustrophobic*
didn't enjoy anything	*fear of crowds*
negative	*memory loss*
critical	*apathetic*
undependable	*withdrawn*
sweaty	*personality change*
indecisive	*fatigued*
hopeless	*nervous*
helpless	*restless*
lack of concentration	*wrung hands*
didn't want noise	*lack of appetite*
didn't want light	*worried*
stammered	*depressed*
sleeplessness	*little Bible,*
paranoid	*little prayer*
guilt	*little soul winning*
fear	*worthless*

These feelings and characteristics coming one right upon
another, of course, can cause you to think you are crazy. To feel
guilty about not being dependable about your work one minute
and to be completely apathetic about your work the next minute
is difficult for the chronically-ill person to understand.

I do not remember ever wanting to take my life, but I did ask
Jesus over and over again to take me home to Heaven. At other
times I remember saying over and over, "Lord Jesus, I long to
be perfectly whole." I was crying for emotional healing.

When the sick person has difficulty even understanding her
own self, friends and relatives surely cannot begin to understand.
Therefore, having the support of my husband and my preacher,

whether or not they understood, probably kept me from further depths in my feelings. My husband told me much later that he always thought I'd come "out of the fog" in which I seemed to be living. During the time, he never acted as if anything were wrong. He accepted me as I was when I could not accept myself as I was.

Thank the Lord for a preacher who makes me laugh. I used to feel as if it would be good for me to just get to the back row of church (slipping in and out as fast as possible) just to laugh. Those were the only times I can remember laughing. I felt I was numb, and, yet, I couldn't have been totally numb to remember so many conflicting feelings.

*Mrs. Evans during
her 1982 chemo*

There were many others who were a great support to me, also. The following paragraph and verses from a preacher friend of ours helped me so much when I was sick.

The Lord has different yardsticks with which to measure the same people at different times. It is not the same when he or she is a teenager, a young adult, a mature leader, or an older adult. It is not the same measure or yardstick when we are sick, afflicted, or laid aside in some way. Just simply operating at 20-30 percent may, in fact, be a great victory in sickness, when in full health it would be laziness and a tragic waste of time and talent. Don't judge yourself. Let the Lord do it. Certainly don't let others do it.

"Let a man so account of us, as of the ministers of Christ, and stewards of the mysteries of God. Moreover it is requited in stewards, that a man be found faithful. But with

me it is a very small thing that I should be judged of you, or of man's judgment: yea, I judge not mine own self. For I know nothing by myself; yet am I not hereby justified: but he that judgeth me is the Lord." (I Corinthians 4:1-4)

I am well aware of the fact that I am opening myself to possible criticism by writing all of these things. After counting the possible cost, I could not give up the burden for the people I see, both men and women, going through chronic illness or the aftermath of some treatment or problem. Their not being able to tell what's wrong with them, not being understood that much by the medical community, and not being able to reach out to anyone nor to let anyone reach in to them is horrendous. A well-known evangelist told audiences that he sometimes doubted his salvation while going through "shades of hell" with his chemotherapy treatments. His words were used to give me great comfort and encouragement. They helped me so very much through the months ahead.

When my doctor at Mayo Clinic told me, "You vill bloom again," I remained hopeful.

Many losses—health, loved ones, jobs and many other things—seem to manifest themselves in similar ways. If I could help you by admitting the feelings I had to fight, I am willing to do so. By the way, because of medical progress, chemotherapy, though still a very difficult circumstance, was so much easier this last time than when I took it in 1982.

Please don't give up on yourself or your loved one—even if it is a decade or two! Just tell your loved one that she is doing great no matter how little you think she is doing. She probably is doing the best she can. She desperately wants someone to believe in her when she cannot even believe in herself.

What About You?

Now, what about you, the one who is left lonely or feeling rejected by the sick person? Once you realize the sick or recuperating loved one is doing the best she can, be sure you take care of yourself. If you don't, you will join the ranks of the sick and afflicted yourself. Have several people who can help encourage you and will do so whether or not you think you are doing well. Taking pressure off yourself will help you in your attitude toward yourself and the one for whom you are caring.

Remember, God is the **only** One Who can go all the way through the valley with you! *"For he hath said, I will never leave thee, nor forsake thee."* (Hebrews 13:5b)

CHAPTER THIRTEEN

"YOU VILL BLOOM AGAIN!"

F ROM TIME TO time something happens to remind me
of the wonderful words, "You vill bloom again!" God
used these words to help me hold on in some pretty bleak
months following chemotherapy treatment.

After my first bout with cancer and chemotherapy, there
came the day when I decided I should give up trying to work
as both Dean of Women and a faculty member at Hyles-
Anderson College. Not wanting to make that drastic decision
before checking out all possibilities for help, I went to see my
coordinating doctor at Mayo Clinic.

Dr. Frigas asked me questions about my family such as,
"Are your children gone from home?" "When does your
husband leave for work?" "When does your husband get
home in the evenings?" "Are you the type to putter around
the house all day alone?"

Answering these questions helped me realize it would
probably be more hurtful for me to be home alone than to
continue working. However, knowing I could not face all the
administrative duties made me say, "But, Dr. Frigas, I'm
hurting my workers."

CANCER: MY ENEMY, MY FRIEND

He immediately answered, "You vill bloom again."

That doctor will never know what his encouraging words did for me. I didn't get better all at once. However, every time I began to doubt if I would ever be well again, I'd think "I vill bloom again."

Let me tell you about this amazing physician who encourages me every time I see him. Dr. Frigas is from Greece and knows four or five languages. He doesn't seem to mind my quoting his words with accent! So many times we could help one another with a word like "vill" that could be an apple of gold in a picture of silver. *"A word fitly spoken is like apples of gold in pictures of silver."* (Proverbs 25:11)

Dr. Frigas did not act is if there wasn't a real problem. He did not act as if I were not doing my best. As a doctor, he simply gave beautiful words that helped a patient on her long journey which sometimes seemed so lonely. Thank God for a doctor who was used to give good words!

CHAPTER FOURTEEN

MY SUPPORT GROUP = MY CHURCH

IN THE PAGES of our local newspaper, there are sometimes 20 or more support groups listed such as, but not limited to, Alcoholics Anonymous, drug abuse and addiction organizations, and support groups that have to do with cancer, diabetes, tobacco, gambling, overeating and divorce. These groups, to some extent, are doing a good work, I'm sure.

For instance, an "ostomy" group gives much help to patients in learning how to handle their new paraphernalia, how to order supplies, and how to manage in new routines. Medicines, insurance possibilities, and all such needs can be discussed at the meetings.

"Y-Me" is a support group for breast cancer patients. I was invited to attend their get-togethers many times. However, I never entertained a thought of attending. I got to wondering why I didn't go. It was then I realized I have, and have had for many years, an all-inclusive support group that has helped me, not only through cancer and chemotherapy, but through all of the testing that has come my way. My support group? It is a fundamental, local, King James Bible-believing, soul-winning New Testament Baptist Church!

My Support Group Leader

My pastor of my church is my support group leader. First Peter 5:2-4 describes my pastor to a "T." *"Feed the flock of God which is among you, taking the oversight thereof, not by constraint, but willingly; not for filthy lucre, but of a ready mind; Neither as being lords over God's heritage, but being ensamples to the flock. And when the chief Shepherd shall appear, ye shall receive a crown of glory that fadeth not away."*

Our support group leader seems to stay awake nights just to think about what to do for our group. He studies hours and hours in order to give that which helps us to go out to live better, more fulfilling and more productive lives.

He has been known to do research into how to help individual members of our group. A friend told me, "Preacher asked, 'What does Mrs. Evans need from her pastor while she's sick?' " I have said many times that my preacher, Dr. Jack Hyles, has "coached" me through this last bout of cancer, surgery and chemotherapy.

He helps us know how to do good in order to achieve and to earn eternal rewards. He certainly does *"...provoke unto love and to good works."* (Hebrews 10:24)

The Support Group

All the people who believe and practice Hebrews 10:25 which says, *"Not forsaking the assembling of ourselves together, as the manner of some is; but exhorting one another: and so much the more as ye see the day approaching,"* are in my group. They exhort me while loving me as they *"see the day approaching."*

They are more than support group fellow members. They are my brothers and sisters in Christ. Acts 2:42 tells us, *"And they continued stedfastly in the apostles' doctrine and fellowship, and in breaking of bread, and in prayers,"* and that is what I have in my church.

Sometimes we disagree, just as in any support group, but we have a plan to help us work through problems between us. *"Let nothing be done through strife or vainglory; but in lowliness of mind let each esteem other better than themselves. Look not every man on his own things, but every man also on the things of others. Let this mind be in you, which was also in Christ Jesus."* (Philippians 2:3-5)

The Material

Most support groups have books, manuals, tapes and other materials available to its members. We have manuals and books and tapes, too. However, we have **the Book—the Bible.** Our Source Book, the Bible, is so inexhaustible that no one has ever run out of material on any problem.

Studying the Bible can be done from childhood to death without having to search for any other material on how to live or how to handle sickness, death, loneliness or any other hurt or problem. *"But continue thou in the things which thou hast learned and hast been assured of, knowing of whom thou hast learned them; And that from a child thou hast known the holy scriptures, which are able to make thee wise unto salvation through faith which is in Christ Jesus. All scripture is given by inspiration of God, and is profitable for doctrine, for reproof, for correction, for instruction in righteousness: That the man of God may be perfect, throughly furnished unto all good works.* " (II Timothy 3:14-17)

The following is some "material" expressly for the support of the dying:

"Let not your heart be troubled: ye believe in God, believe also in me. In my Father's house are many mansions: if it were not so, I would have told you. I go to prepare a place for you. And if I go and prepare a place for you, I will come again, and receive you unto myself; that where I am, there ye may be also. And wither I go ye know, and the way ye know. Thomas saith unto him, Lord, we know not whither thou goest; and how can we know the way? Jesus saith unto him, I am the way, the truth, and the life: no man cometh unto the Father, but by me. If ye had known me, ye should have known my Father also: and from henceforth ye know him, and have seen him." (John 14:1-7)

"And I heard a voice from heaven saying unto me, Write, Blessed are the dead which die in the Lord from henceforth: Yea, saith the Spirit, that they may rest from their labours; and their works do follow them." (Revelation 14:13)

"And said, Naked came I out of my mother's womb, and naked shall I return thither: the LORD gave, and the LORD hath taken away; blessed be the name of the LORD." (Job 1:21)

"Precious in the sight of the LORD is the death of his saints." (Psalm 116:15)

"We are confident, I say, and willing rather to be absent from the body, and to be present with the Lord." (II Corinthians 5:8)

"Jesus said unto her, I am the resurrection, and the life: he that believeth in me, though he were dead, yet shall he live: And whosoever liveth and believeth in me shall never die. Believest thou this?" (John 11:25, 26)

"For to me to live is Christ, and to die is gain." (Philippians 1:21)

"And the peace of God, which passeth all understanding, shall keep your hearts and minds through Christ Jesus." (Philippians 4:7)

"Casting all your care upon him; for he careth for you." (I Peter 5:7)

"And God shall wipe away all tears from their eyes; and there shall be no more death, neither sorrow, nor crying, neither shall there be any more pain: for the former things are passed away." (Revelation 21:4)

Take time to also read Psalm 23, I Corinthians 15, and I Thessalonians 4:14-18.

The following is some "material" from *the Source Book* for those who are sick:

"The LORD will strengthen him upon the bed of languishing: Thou wilt make all his bed in his sickness." (Psalm 41:3)

129

"It is good for me that I have been afflicted; that I might learn thy statutes." (Psalm 119:71)

"That the trial of your faith, being much more precious than gold that perisheth, though it be tried with fire, might be found unto praise and honour and glory at the appearing of Jesus Christ." (I Peter 1:7)

"Jesus answered, Neither hath this man sinned, nor his parents: but that the works of God should be made manifest in him." (John 9:3)

"When Jesus heard that, he said, This sickness is not unto death, but for the glory of God, that the Son of God might be glorified thereby." (John 11:4)

"Though he were a Son, yet learned he obedience by the things which he suffered." (Hebrews 5:8)

"Behold, we count them happy which endure. Ye have heard of the patience of Job, and have seen the end of the Lord: that the Lord is very pitiful, and of tender mercy." (James 5:11)

Please read II Corinthians 12:7-10 and Romans 8:16-18.

The following is some "material" particularly for the support of the fearful:

"And Moses said unto the people, Fear ye not, stand still, and see the salvation of the LORD, which he will shew to you to day: for the Egyptians whom ye have seen to day, ye shall see them again no more forever. The LORD shall fight for you, and ye shall hold your peace." (Exodus 14:13, 14)

"Only rebel not ye against the LORD, neither fear ye the people of the land; for they are bread for us: their defence is departed from thee, and the LORD is with us: fear them not." (Numbers 14:9)

"Fear not, neither be discouraged." (Deuteronomy 1:21b)

"And the LORD said unto Joshua, Fear not, neither be thou dismayed." (Joshua 8:1a)

"Say to them that are of a fearful heart, Be strong, fear not: behold, your God will come with vengeance, even God with a recompense; he will come and save you." (Isaiah 35:4)

"Fear thou not; for I am with thee: be not dismayed; for I am thy God: I will strengthen thee; yea, I will help thee; yea, I will uphold thee with the right hand of my righteousness." (Isaiah 41:10)

"Hearken unto me, ye that know righteousness, the people in whose heart is my law; fear ye not the reproach of men, neither be ye afraid of their revilings." (Isaiah 51:7)

"Fear ye not therefore, ye are of more value than many sparrows." (Matthew 10:31)

"Fear not, little flock; for it is your Father's good pleasure to give you the kingdom." (Luke 12:32)

The following is some "material" for the support of those who are brokenhearted:

"This poor man cried, and the LORD heard him, and saved him out of his troubles." (Psalm 34:6)

"The righteous cry, and the LORD heareth, and delivereth them out of all their troubles. The LORD is nigh unto them that are of a broken heart; and saveth such as be of a contrite spirit. Many are the afflictions of the righteous: but the LORD delivereth him out of them all." (Psalm 34:17-19)

"...Weeping may endure for a night, but joy cometh in the morning." (Psalm 30:5)

"Blessed are ye that hunger now: for ye shall be filled. Blessed are ye that weep now: for ye shall laugh." (Luke 6:21)

"Let not your heart be troubled: ye believe in God, believe also in me." (John 14:1)

My Support Group Prayer

I thank You, Lord, for my church, which has been a support group of all support groups to me. Thank You for a place I can continue to learn to be:

Firm, but not harsh;
Realistic, but not skeptical;
Scheduled, but not rigid;
Pure, but not proud;
Closed-mouthed, but not unfriendly;
Appropriate, but not stiff;
Funny, but not frivolous;
Teachable, but not gullible;
Flexible, but not scatter-brained;
Humble, but not super pious;
Kind, but not compromising;

MY SUPPORT GROUP = MY CHURCH

Dependable, but not stubborn;
Persistent, but not needling;
Precise, but not picky;
Simple, but not foolish;
Demanding, but not intolerant;
Thorough, but not unkind;
Human, but not worldly;
Generous, but not irresponsible;
Spiritual, but not impractical;
Enthusiastic, but not "hyper";
Honest, but not brutal;
Fair, but not unloving;
Proper, but not unreal;
Confident, but not snobbish;
Bold, but not brazen;
Busy, but not harried;
Efficient, but not hurried;
Active, but not shallow;
Deep, but not dry;
Wise, but not intimidating;
Intense, but not forbidding;
Empathetic, but not uncontrolled;
Forgiving, but not naive;
Sympathetic, but not pitying;
Helpful, but not condescending;
Penitent, but not paralyzed;
Organized, but not bossy;
Spontaneous, but not inconsistent.

Lord, I guess I am asking to grow in favor with God and man. I am asking You to help me become a balanced person. Amen.

God's plan, which is always the best plan, is not for us to get our counseling, encouragement and help from the unsaved world. *"Blessed is the man that walketh not in the counsel of the ungodly, nor standeth in the way of sinners, nor sitteth in the seat of the scornful."* (Psalm 1:1) God's plan is for us to get our counseling, encouragement and help from a local New Testament church, our pastor, the people of that church and His Word, the Bible. He also intends for us to be a part of that support group and be a help to others. Let me urge you, if you are not already doing so, to become a part of a support group as I have described.

CHAPTER FIFTEEN

MY CIRCLE OF PROTECTION

THE IDEA OF having a circle of protection came to me during July and August of 1981. I wrote the thoughts for "Circle of Protection" in June of 1982.

I recall reading my notes on "Circle of Protection" while taking it easy after my first mastectomy. My heart was filled with joy to think that the Lord had been preparing me for a loss since cancer had possibly already begun its work in my body when I was writing in 1981.

I can honestly say that God gave and continues to give me a circle of protection. I have shed a few tears over God's goodness to me as I've been touched by people's care for me, but, as far as I know, I haven't shed a tear or lost a moment of sleep over my operation, the treatments we're beginning, or anything else connected with this operation.

I do know my circle of protection has thus far done just what my thoughts written two months before surgery said it would do—it protected me. Most every thing and every person I named in my circle were available when I needed them.

A week from the day of surgery, a mini-spectacular was scheduled for Tampa, Florida. I determined not to cancel the meeting as the pastor was counting on me. People I love made it possible for me to travel to that meeting. Once I was there, I enjoyed speaking from a recliner which the kind people had arranged for me. My arm was propped up with a pillow. I felt great! Though I would not encourage someone to go out before she should, for me, it surely beat sitting at home looking at a scar.

Folks have told me, "There are women who just fall apart over this operation." I'm not proud that I haven't so far. I'm thankful. Praise the Lord! His grace truly is sufficient!

Let Me Share My Circle of Protection with You!

One day when I was playing in the sand at the Indiana Dunes State Park, I built a castle of sorts and fashioned a circle of protection around it. Moats around castles always fascinated me.

As I looked at it, God seemed to say, "Marlene, that's just how I have provided for you. You have to take advantage of your circle of protection I've made for you."

It was a wonderfully sweet lesson to me. He has given me hundreds of people, thousands of trees, birds, animals, sunrises and sunsets, and all kinds of work and activity with which to encircle and protect myself from emotional deprivation or depression.

MY CIRCLE OF PROTECTION

I imagined myself as the castle and began to think of the people and things of life as the grains of sand piled around the castle (me). It says in Romans 8:35-39 that **nothing** can separate us from the love of God, which shows me that nothing can separate me from God's circle of protection in my life.

My circle of protection includes: Wendell L. Evans, Psalm 23, redbirds, Dad and Hazel, oak trees, John 14:1-7, teaching, strawberries, my preacher, Queen Anne's lace, maple trees, the United States of America, Deep River Park, Joy Evans Ryder, David Evans, Cracker Barrel, weeping willows, Annie Ruth McGuire, Mayo Clinic, sunsets, blue buntings, Lake Michigan, Philippians 4:4-8, Beth Emery, goldfinches, Dianne Smith Dowdey, Arlys Cooper, The Great Smoky Mountains, Philippians 3:10, Hyles-Anderson College students, Mrs. Beverly Hyles, Isaiah 1:18, Mike Smith, Jim Emery, The Romans' Road, Kathryn Emery, Proverbs 31, my house, writing, Loretta Walker, Isaiah 41:10, Psalm 47, red-winged blackbirds, Psalm 91, John 3:16, Leslie Simpson Beaman, blue jays, Romans 8:26-28, Dr. Viola Walden, mourning doves, Hyles-Anderson College co-workers, tulips, Dick Emery, Proverbs 3:5,6, Jerry Smith, Titus 2:1-8, fresh garden vegetables, "1812 Overture," "I Would Love to Tell You What I Think of Jesus," dogwoods, winning a soul to Christ, Kris Grafton, Psalm 19, being allowed to help God work a miracle, "Clair de Lune," lilies of the valley, Linda Meister, azaleas, quilts, violets, Christmas, watermelons, Edith Boyd, teaching "Women Used of God," goldenrod, my grandchildren, Rudy Atwood's piano tapes, grits with my eggs, North Carolina, Carol Frye, sitting in newly cut grass, the Bible on cassette, Vicki Mitchell, cantaloupe, fried chicken, Faulkners, candles (lit), "William Tell Overture," Linda Stubblefield, warm popcorn, speaking, Psalm 147:3, poached eggs, Susie Taylor, Tennessee, childhood stories, JoJo Moffitt, Hebrews 13:5,6, "Jesus, Jesus, There's Something About that Name," Jane Grafton, memories of Bob Jones University, Robersons, sunrises, Nebraska, snow on pine and fir trees, Pat Hays Hehn, standing in a soft warm rain, Psalm 100, recycling greeting cards, popping corn, fireplaces, my birthday, Mary Purdum and counseling.

I could write at least 10,000 other things, situations and people, not to mention **good memories**, God has given to recall when I want a circle of protection. For instance, I don't believe I even mentioned books I love to read.

Your Circle of Protection Would Be Different from Mine!

If I had shut my mouth and kept my body still as a child, I would have piano playing, quilting, sewing, embroidering, tatting, and other abilities in my circle of protection. Mom tried, but I won. Except, I lost. I'd love to have some of those things in my circle now.

How often I've heard people say, "I just sit down and play the piano for my enjoyment and relaxation. It soothes me." You see, that is in their circles. At one time or another, it can help ease their hurt, anger, nerves, depression and worry.

My mom is no longer in my circle, but, oh, the memories and all that she left with me! When she went to be with the Lord, it hurt (a lot), but I didn't fall apart. She had taught me to love the Bible and appreciate things and people, and so they were there when she left. They didn't take her place; there was a gap, but I turned to see so much around me. It helped!

MY CIRCLE OF PROTECTION

You'll notice my circle of protection might be different from that of a young person. My own circle is startlingly different from what it would have been before I was 35 years of age. Because of degenerative disc disease and subsequent back surgeries, I can only walk short distances and do not care to stand in one place or do much of anything else (work or fun activities) which requires physical effort. As housework, picking berries, cucumbers and tomatoes, running, cycling, and the 100 other things a very physically, active person does left my circle of protection, other things took on greater importance.

I didn't die just because my lifestyle had to change. I have a "pity party" over it about once a year, but I keep turning to look at the circle of protection God has given me.

I don't wonder what or who will go next. I just try to develop all the activities, people and things I can and let God take care of what is taken from my circle of protection.

For some, it will be eyes. For Keith Frye, it was eyes, ears, speech, and the whole body

Mrs. Evans interviewing Keith at the Spectacular

within weeks, in that order, as he developed a severe case of Multiple Sclerosis. As his ears (hearing) returned, he enjoyed listening to tapes, a talking bird, and people reading to him. Much had been taken from Keith's circle of protection, but by the time he went to Heaven, he had added many things to his circle. Keith had someone feed him, people who visited him, a family who stood by him, books, tapes, music and a place to stay. Best of all, he had Jesus to talk to whenever he wanted. He began depending on Him so much more.

It's sorta' your decision. You can lose your faith in one friend or a preacher, you can see a tragedy come to your son or daughter or you can lose your mom or dad and declare, "It's all over." Or you can say, "There's a gap that can never be filled, but I'll turn and turn and turn to see all God has given me for a circle of protection."

Develop your circle now before you lose something major like your job, your daughter, your friend or your eyes. It's the way to *"Rejoice in the Lord alway: and again I say, Rejoice."* (Philippians 4:4)

CHAPTER SIXTEEN

SHOULD YOU BE READING THE BIBLE TO SOMEONE?

W HEN I WAS first married, I remember hearing of someone being so sick that he didn't even want to read the Bible. The young husband whose wife was discussing this circumstance was known to love the Word of God and...so...I wondered. As a "knowledgeable" young bride in her early twenties, I determined that he needed the Bible even more when he was physically weak.

The last few years I have been reading the Bible through each year, as well as do what I call my "fun reading." "Fun reading" is not study or duty reading. It's usually from Psalms, Proverbs and Philippians because I like to devour my favorites. It has distressed me a great deal that I haven't always kept up with my reading during my chemotherapy days. Some days I didn't care if I read anything. My eyes didn't even seem to focus correctly. Neither did I care to eat food, drink water, talk to my loved ones, or do anything else some days. Some days I didn't know if I wanted to stay in bed, get up, walk, sit, listen to music, write or go someplace...I was just a mess not knowing which way to turn.

Now, times like these are surely when I need the Bible to settle me, wouldn't you think? And then, God allowed some good news to come to me one day when several people offered to sit and read the Bible out loud to me. They read the Bible to me even if I didn't seem to be responding. It couldn't have been too thrilling for them as they read Exodus and Leviticus to a "zombie." But, oh, how it helped me! Just knowing that I was not going to lose my reading the Bible through in a year was a comfort to me.

Brother Hyles has often said that when water is poured through a strainer not much remains, but the strainer is cleaner. Sometimes I didn't understand or retain much of what was being read to me, but I believe I was cleaner because it went through me. Some days I didn't have a very long attention span, but someone would put a Bible tape in my recorder and that heavy loud voice would come through to me once in a while. A verse would get into my heart and make me glad. I must admit, there were times I didn't even want to hear the voice coming from the tape recorder, but in the end it always helped me.

I recall talking about these feelings to my friend, the late Nancy Perry, who suffered so terribly with rheumatoid arthritis. She told me that she experienced the same type of feelings in not wanting to read the Bible or do anything else for that matter. She said, "I used to hear people say they didn't feel like reading the Bible when they were sick, and I just figured they were backslidden. But, I've changed my mind on that—along with a lot of other things!"

My Aunt Lela, who passed away several years ago, had

been very sick with extreme blood pressure problems as well as severe pain in her legs. I thought, "I wonder if she, too (a Bible reader) has not felt like reading the Bible?" When I discussed my feelings with her, she answered, "Oh, Marlene, I haven't taken an interest in anything. I just walk the floor day and night trying to get relief." The day I called her was one of my good days so I carefully chose a short portion of Scripture and called back to see if I could read to her. She said, "Oh, I'd like that." She had a restful night for the first time in many days.

I have come to the startling conclusion that the very times we **most** need the Bible, we're often too weak or too medicated to know how to get it. Therefore, why don't you think of someone to whom you could say, "Do you mind if I share a few verses of Scripture?"

I can promise you from personal experience that you would be giving them the best gift of all—God's Word!

CHAPTER SEVENTEEN

BRINGING BACK THE SICK

TODAY I WAS talking with a person who had experienced her first day back at work after a week or so of sickness. She said, "Mrs. Evans, they didn't even ask me how I was. They just started asking me questions they'd apparently been saving for me for the first minute I returned. I just panicked and left for home as soon as possible. I didn't even know the answers to any of their questions."

My mind immediately went back to the months following chemotherapy treatments when I made several false starts back into the office. While lying in bed, I felt perfectly able to return to work. While I was walking around the house where no one expected anything of me, I felt as if I could easily go back to work. Then, after proceeding to the office, I found myself sitting blankly staring at a pile of work about which I felt completely out of control.

I discovered that I was able to teach classes sooner than I was able to go to my desk, out into the halls of my school, or to counsel. The reason for that was that JoJo Moffitt, my assistant teacher, cleared away class business for me and prepared the class for me by letting me enter after the class started and leave before it was finished. This allowed me to "feel" my way back into things on my own time table. When I was up before the class, I had notes I knew well. I was not placed in a position where I was caught "off guard." If I could not have made my "comeback" gradually, I don't know when I could have ever gotten back to work.

If a person has a job to which they cannot make a gradual re-entry, I would advise her to test herself carefully before she goes back and has to leave again or makes poor judgments or "shows herself" to unfeeling (or just plain ignorant) people through tears or anger.

The "shower test" is a good test to take before going back to work. A few days with the flu can leave you feeling pretty good one morning. Before you declare yourself well, take a shower. You might be so weak that you crawl into bed not even having the strength to dress for work.

If you have a job which requires you to go back in full force for eight hours a day, test yourself on two hour special projects and work up to eight hours as quickly as you are able to before going back on the job.

If you feel as if you're ignorant on how to help people come back after accidents, sickness or operations, ask God to help you learn before you have to experience a time like this first hand in order to be understanding.

The only time in all my years of working on a job that I ever got into a serious human relations problem was the time I went back to teaching one week earlier than the doctor had advised following surgery. After all, I was feeling great, getting a permanent, and doing other activities where I wasn't likely to be crossed by anyone. Nervous systems aren't the same for a long time after being put to sleep for the simplest of operations.

If you can help someone make a "comeback," here are some things you might try:

• **Give the person a re-entry time.** No matter how busy you are and no matter how much you've needed the absent person, it will be to your benefit to de-program her just as an astronaut is de-programmed when he comes back from outer space.

Don't just say, "Hi! You're doing fine, huh? Glad you're back. Let's get going." The fact is, the sick one should come back as a non-complaining employee, but she secretly wishes someone would try to really understand.

• **Program the person to take time to just sit at her desk or working place and brief herself or get briefed on what has gone on in her absence.** Now of course, I am well aware of the fact that there are jobs I've had, such as waitressing, pinning play clothes together at a factory, and picking fruit and vegetables in a truck garden, which would be difficult to handle in this way. I do remember, though, going to work in a dime store having broken ribs. The supervisor let me sit on a high stool at the cash register and go home early.

But let's go back to the desk. Sometimes a person feels they are doing well just to find the desk the first day back!

• **If at all possible, count the person absent (in your**

mind) her first day back. Just for your own sake, if for no one else's, bring her back right. It may save many working hours, and possibly, it will save you a good worker. I've watched sick people work not at all or part-time for several years only to make a beautiful "comeback" to work another decade or two for the organization that gave them time.

• **If a person says she is sick, believe her!** If you believe people who say they are sick, you'll be glad you did! I've worked with many colleagues who have tried to diagnose the illness of their co-workers as "only emotional." Later, they've had to admit that leukemia, severe diabetes, brain tumors and rheumatoid arthritis isn't "only emotional." It is usually more than emotional, but if it were "just emotional," that might be the worst of all. There are a good many people who are thrilled to get a bad diagnosis from a doctor because somewhere along the line someone had caused them to think their sickness wasn't believed.

This point brings to mind a situation that occurred when I was a young full-time teacher in the public school system of Greenville, South Carolina. I watched a still younger educational star appear on the horizon in the form of a Bob Jones University student teacher. She absolutely "burned up the woods" as she organized her first graders, decorated her room, and turned in a performance par excellence in every other teaching area! Of course, she was hired to be a full-time teacher the following year.

Even though I was a tad jealous (probably an understatement) and felt a bit threatened, I was not happy when I saw the girl return to do nothing as a paid full-time teacher. It was startling; it was spooky. The "fireball" had become a "tortoise" during one summer's time. The "creator of all the creativity" could not seem to think of one new idea. The one who had so gallantly shunned the lineup of lazy teachers sitting on the chairs at the side of the playground now sat on a chair most all day.

Out of my great storehouse of knowledge, wisdom and experience came the obvious conclusion: "She put on a good show to get a good grade in student teaching and now doesn't give a care as long as she's on a payroll." A first-rate detective, lawyer or doctor wouldn't be caught dead calling a decision with such scant detail, but I rushed in where angels would fear to tread. I had seen and I had heard; I made my judgment!

To add insult to injury, the young lady began asking me to take her to the doctor. She said she wasn't feeling well, and, in my feeble thinking, I pronounced her "lazy." So I prescribed work for her which I felt would cure anything. After so many times of "being taken advantage of," I told her she could catch a bus from the doctor's office so I could drop her and go on my way. I highly resented the whole deal.

A few weeks later I was called to a hospital to visit her. She was experiencing such things as bleeding after just knocking her toe against the end of the bed. Yes, you guessed it! The "lazy," "no-care," "take-advantage" girl soon died! And the diagnosis—leukemia! I spent five or six days agonizing as I've never before or since agonized. I wasn't tortured over a friend going to be with Jesus; I was in torment over my guilt in being hatefully and selfishly judgmental.

Now, I know God dealt with me in an unusually dramatic way (God sometimes has to hit me over the head to get my attention!), and certainly I realize that we can't go running to take everyone to the doctor in case the diagnosis is leukemia, but a loving heart will cause us to reserve judgment and to help each person find a way to meet her needs!

If I had been a steady individual who stayed by people, I would have been her friend when she was a fantastic teacher (even if my pride hurt) or when she was a bad teacher (lazy or sick). Laziness is something that needs to be fixed just as much as a physical illness, and if I'm a Christian, I'm to be in the "people-fixin' business." Right? We tend to think we are justified in turning aside from a lazy person, but we are responsible to stand by the terminally ill. This, of course, is some more of our human reasoning and is certainly not God's way.

Remember, *"And of some have compassion, making a difference."* (Jude 22)

CHAPTER EIGHTEEN

WHEN GOOD PEOPLE SUFFER

T HE AGE-OLD QUESTION, "Why do some good people seem to suffer more than bad people?" shows that we still believe deep down that we can make a deal with God.

When we say at a funeral, "If anyone is in Heaven, it's this good lady," we once again display our need for believing in doing so many good works for Heaven instead of once and for all knowing that *"For by grace are ye saved through faith; and that not of yourselves: it is the gift of God: Not of works, lest any man should boast."* (Ephesians 2:8, 9) There is no dealing with God in exchanging works for Heaven.

Neither is there any dealing with God for being a good enough Christian that we can play "Let's Make a Deal" to keep bad things from happening. The whole book of Job is a wonderful explanation of reasons why good men suffer. When Job felt so alone and couldn't seem to find God anywhere, he said something that to this day is quoted and sung to help other Christians. Job 23:10 says, *"But he knoweth the way that I take: when he hath tried me, I shall come forth as gold.*" This verse is a great summation of why good people suffer.

*"And the L*ORD *said unto Satan, Hast thou considered my servant Job, that there is none like him in the earth, a perfect and an upright man, one that feareth God, and escheweth evil? Then Satan answered the L*ORD*, and said, Doth Job fear God for nought? Hast not thou made an hedge about him, and about his house, and about all that he hath on every side? thou hast blessed the work of his hands, and his substance is increased in the land. But put forth thy hand now, and touch all that he hath, and he will curse thee to thy face."* (Job 1:8-11)

These verses show that Satan himself thought godly people would curse God when their "Let's-Make-a-Deal" approach to living a righteous life didn't **seem** to pay off.

In Job 42:12a we find that *"So the Lord blessed the latter end of Job more than his beginning."*

People who have eyes so fixed on money, health, houses, lands and things might be able to understand God's goodness when everything comes out all right in the end here in this world as it seemed to with Job. But, what about the times when the good Christian seems to die without justice being done in the world's eye?

The John 9 account of the man blind from his birth is understandable. Jesus answered a question about this blind man by saying, *"...Neither hath this man sinned, nor his parents: but that the works of God should be made manifest in him."* (John 9:3) Then Jesus chose to heal this blind man in John 9:6, 7 which say, *"When he had thus spoken, he spat on the ground, and made clay of the spittle, and he anointed the eyes of the blind man with the clay, and said unto him, "Go wash in the pool of Siloam, (which is by interpretation, Sent.) He went his way therefore, and washed, and came seeing."*

That the works of God be made manifest is a good reason for suffering! But, what about the blind who are not healed on this earth? Psalm 73:3 says what man thinks so often, *"For I was envious at the foolish, when I saw the prosperity of the wicked."* Psalm 73:12 continues, *"Behold, these are the ungodly, who prosper in the world; they increase in riches."* Now look at Psalm 73:17 which says, *"Until I went into the sanctuary of God; then understood I their end. Surely thou didst set them in slippery places: thou castedst them down into destruction. How are they brought into desolation, as in a moment! they are utterly consumed with terrors. As a dream when one awaketh; so, O LORD, when thou awakest, thou shalt despise their image. Thus my heart was grieved, and I was pricked in my reins. So foolish was I, and ignorant: I was as a beast before thee. Nevertheless I am continually with thee: thou hast holden me by my right hand. Thou shalt guide me with thy counsel, and afterward receive me to glory. Whom have I in heaven but thee? and there is not upon earth that I desire beside thee. My flesh and my heart faileth: but God is the strength of my heart, and my portion for ever. For, lo, they that are far from thee shall perish: thou hast destroyed all them that go a whoring from thee. But it is good for me to draw near to God: I have put my trust in the LORD God, that I may declare all thy works."*

To think that no matter how low we are brought, He will help us is such a great comfort. *"The LORD preserveth the simple: I was brought low, and he helped me."* (Psalm 116:6) How sad it would be to go through life never knowing the mercy and help of the Lord. No amount of prosperity in this world would be worth that.

"It is good for me that I have been afflicted; that I might learn thy statutes." (Psalm 119:71) Wouldn't it be worth having afflictions if it took that affliction to learn His Word? *"That I may know him, and the power of his resurrection, and the fellowship of his sufferings, being made conformable unto his death,"* (Philippians 3:10) indicates that fellowshipping with His sufferings will help us know Him better.

I Timothy 6:6-10 are great verses which help us understand that prosperity might not be what some of us could handle. *"But godliness with contentment is great gain. For we brought nothing into this world, and it is certain we can carry nothing out. And having food and raiment let us be therewith content. But they that will be rich fall into temptation and a snare, and into many foolish and hurtful lusts, which drown men in destruction and perdition. For the love of money is the root of all evil: which while some coveted after, they have erred from the faith, and pierced themselves through with many sorrows."* The Word of God is so full of truths that would forever settle this question that I wonder if we just fail to read and know its truths. What we are dealing with should no longer even be a question in the mind of a mature believer.

CHAPTER NINETEEN

ARE YOU WORTH MORE THAN YOUR DOG?

"**I** AM NOT GOING to run to a doctor every time I have an ache or a pain."

"I'm no baby; I can tough it out."

"All those doctors want is your money anyway."

"I can get well just as quickly doctoring myself."

"There's nothing wrong with me I can't take care of with an aspirin."

Have you heard any of the above statements until you've been brainwashed into believing them all 100 percent? Are these statements an over-reaction to hypochondria, that is, reacting against the person who wants to give you an "organ recital" every time she sees you?

Or, perhaps we hear those statements as a "hangover" from the "good ole days" when there were very few doctors in certain areas. In those times, there was nothing to do but diagnose and treat ourselves or be stoical about pain and hope for the best.

In these days of medical centers, specialists, tests, and ample health insurance for at least thousands and thousands of the people of our country, many still say, "Let's wait it out."

I've watched fellow workers "wait out" weeks of pain from an abscessed tooth and still have to go on antibiotics before having treatment by a dentist. When they finally give in, they and everyone around them gets relief within a day or two. If a person doesn't have dental insurance, it's still just not right to mope around work or snap at everyone in sight for a week if a person has any money at all. Sometimes the person in pain goes out and buys a piece of furniture or a new dress but says they have no money for the dentist. Others won't go to a dental school where they are charged according to their ability to pay "because that would be taking charity." These people evidentally don't know they're taking charity by wasting much of their time and sometimes the time of others by their moodiness, apathy or unkindness.

Christians are children of the King. Our bodies are the temple of the Holy Spirit, and the temple needs to be kept in repair. If Christians are soul winners, they are the most important people in the whole world.

Soul winners help people learn how to accept Jesus Christ as their personal Saviour to take away their sins and take them to Heaven when they die! Soul winners need to be as alive, alert and as well as is humanly possible. God has given us brains and doctors.

Sometimes ladies go around the house half-croaked with

a headache. When they mention it, someone kindly asks, "Have you taken a Tylenol?" to which they answer, "I don't take medicine." Well, that's just fine, and I admire people who read the Bible, eat, sleep, exercise, live right, think Philippians 4:8 thoughts, drink water, and all those good things in such a way that they seldom have a headache. However, if the lady is dragging and nagging very long, she surely would be doing her family a favor by trying a little Tylenol or whatever helps her at least once in a while.

I've listened to numerous cancer stories since my breast and lymph node cancer was discovered in August 1982. Most of the stories begin with one of these statements, "I missed a checkup." "I never had checkups." "My doctor cancelled an appointment when he went out of town, and I forgot to reschedule." "I knew something wasn't right, but I was afraid to get it checked."

If you are a Christian, you don't own your body. Your body was purchased by the Lord Jesus Christ. You owe Him to live for Him as well and as long as is in His perfect will. You say, "I'm not that good a Christian." If you are a Christian at all, you're adding a little bit of salt to this ole world just by naming His name in the right way.

If your feet give you much trouble, there are podiatrists. If you are prone to sinus trouble, there are remedies to have ready, and on and on it goes. Study the doctors and their specialties in your yellow pages. Go to a major medical center. Your insurance is as good there as any place.

If you don't want to maintain your body as well as you do that of your dog, cat or car, do it first of all for Jesus' sake and then for the sake of those around you.

CANCER: MY ENEMY, MY FRIEND

Pain and uncalled-for fatigue can rob us of at least being able to show the joy of the Lord, and the joy of the Lord is our strength. *"For the joy of the Lord is your strength."* (Nehemiah 8:10b)

CHAPTER TWENTY

HOW TO SAVE YOURSELF FOR CHURCH

W HEN WE DO not feel well, it is very easy to miss church quite often. However, as you read through this book, you will very much see that I realize how important it is for me to get to church even when I am sick—whether it is a result of surgery, chemotherapy, or just my old arthritis acting up.

Because I know the importance of my being in church faithfully to receive the truths my preacher has prayed over, studied for, and given his heart to for his people, I have realized that my faithfulness to church will have to be on purpose. Therefore, I have made a list of things I do to help me, and I trust will help you also. Of course, I realize all these suggestions might not work for you. I hope you will adjust them to fit your situation.

- Prepare your clothing, Bible and offering Wednesday afternoon for Wednesday night church and Saturday afternoon or evening for Sunday church.

- If possible, take a short nap Wednesday and Sunday

afternoons to help you be rested and alert for the services.

- Plan food and medicine so as not to be sick, lethargic or unduly tired. There are medicines that cause you to be dizzy or nauseous. Plan carefully to take these at times that will not interfere with your church attendance.

- Pace activities and rest in order to be the best at church service times. This may mean that you will have to say "no" to people so that you can be in church.

- Be on time.

- Eliminate from your mind all possibility of work or talk during preaching.

- Listen, sing, give, pray and respond appropriately to really experience the service.

- Be careful to be thoughtful of those who sit around you. I can recall times when no one spoke to me. As I analyzed why this might be, I realized that because I was not feeling well, I was not acknowledging those who came around me. I'm sure they felt rejected by me. Therefore, when I am at church, I must greet everyone who crosses my path whether or not I feel like doing so.

- Pray for visitors, those being saved, and those being baptized.

- Choose your seat as carefully as possible, as if you have a very special date. You do!

- As one service ends, start praying for the next one. Ask God to give you exactly what you need. Realize this may be comfort during one service and correction during the next.

"And let us consider one another to provoke unto love and to good works: Not forsaking the assembling of ourselves together, as the manner of some is; but exhorting one another: and so much the more, as ye see the day approaching." (Hebrews 10:24, 25)

CHAPTER TWENTY-ONE

WOULD I TAKE CHEMOTHERAPY AGAIN?

I CANNOT COUNT THE times I have been asked the question, "Would you take chemotherapy again?"

Several years ago, after fielding the question so many times, I felt like it would be helpful to many if I would phrase some thoughts to always have an answer. I have found it interesting as I have read through these thoughts for this book that the suggestions I made then still reflect exactly how I feel today. Yes, I did take chemotherapy **again.** Yes, I did take those treatments at a major medical center. And, yes, I would take chemotherapy yet **again** (for a third time) if my doctors advised me to do so.

The following are those thoughts which became an article for *Christian Womanhood* several years ago.

Of course, I would. God has given men and women the energy, time, money and brains to discover and research the medicines that have been proven to give the best help, and I could not rest comfortably until I started on those medicines God has made available. I feel I owe it to myself, my family and my work to find out what is the best and take it.

Then, if the Lord chooses to take me on Home, I know that it is His will.

I would feel I had done everything I could have done to give more years to finish my work and lay up more rewards in Heaven. (I do so like presents, and I think Heaven is going to be perfection plus presents!) *"Lay not up for yourselves treasures upon earth, where moth and rust doth corrupt, and where thieves break through and steal: But lay up for yourselves treasures in heaven, where neither moth nor rust doth corrupt, and where thieves do not break through nor steal: For where your treasure is, there will your heart be also."* (Matthew 6:20-22)

Now, I wouldn't take chemotherapy on the first recommendation. As soon as I had the facts from the local oncologist, I would go to Mayo Clinic and get their evaluation and recommendation. Because of locality, others might choose to go to M. D. Anderson in Houston, Texas, or Sloane-Kettering in New York City, New York. If I could not go to a major medical institution of this caliber (and I'd be sure I couldn't), I would write or call one of these institutions to see if I could send my tests and slides to them for evaluation. Proverbs 11:14 says, *"...in the multitude of counsellors there is safety."* In a major medical center, a group of doctors observe the same illnesses and symptoms hundreds of times a month, whereas a local practitioner might see a case once in a year.

Then, if both my local oncologist and the experts at a major medical center agreed, I would make my first chemotherapy appointment the minute I received the second recommendation.

Some people say they want to go on to Heaven anyway. The only problem with that thinking is sometimes you don't get to go right away, and chemotherapy might give some better years to you and to those who care for you.

Now, if I were so full of cancer that chemotherapy would only make my last days more miserable, surely the doctors would help me to know that. Undoubtedly the doctors would discuss alternatives to chemotherapy that would make whatever days I had remaining as comfortable as possible for me.

If you have a doctor who will not tell you all the truth you want to know, ask him to refer you to someone who will be able to fully discuss your case with you, i.e, the avenues of treatment, your prognosis, the statistics, the side effects and so forth.

Before asking for a referral, make a list of questions and persistently ask them. More than likely, you **can** convince a doctor that you **want** the truth. Most doctors will usually give you only as much truth as you seem to want. Just be sure you really do want the truth! Some people are more peaceful knowing the truth, and some are more peaceful not knowing what medical science can tell them.

Physicians are reticent about telling patients the full picture for many reasons. Some doctors feel they have failed if the news is less than good; a few cannot be objective as they have become attached to their patients. Many have never dealt with the issue of serious sickness or death for themselves and are not comfortable talking about it. But, numbers of doctors have told the truth only to have their orderly schedules go askew with hysteria, fainting or shock for which they were not prepared.

Perhaps you shouldn't ask too many questions at one time. You can read bushels of books on cancer from libraries and bookstores, and you can call a 1-800 American Cancer Society number listed in most telephone books for help and support.

Some ladies I have talked with do not know whether or not they have had lymph node involvement with a mastectomy. Knowing this can make all the difference in the world. A simple mastectomy is just that—simple—no or very little pain and possibly no need for chemotherapy. If biopsies of lymph nodes under the arm show that cancer has spread to those nodes, then intensive follow-up should be done for many years.

Euphemistic phrases sometimes throw us off. There are those of us who might think the diagnosis of "lymph node involvement" only means the doctors took nodes to check them. "Lymph node involvement" usually, if not always, means there are cancerous lymph nodes present.

On August 6, 1987, I had my fifth year cancer-free anniversary. My first mastectomy, which was the one with lymph node cancer, took place on that date in 1982. On this day at Mayo Clinic (usually your insurance works there as good or better than any place), I asked many questions. From the answers to those questions, I understood that:

- With the number of cancerous lymph nodes I had, I had a 30 percent possibility of not having a recurrence.

- I had a 70 percent possibility of having a recurrence.

- I may or may not be in the 30 percent group of not having a recurrence.

- If I'm not in the 30 percent group, God can move me into that category if He so chooses.

- If I have a recurrence, there is a possibility of fighting off cancer again.

- I cannot count myself cancer-free from the original cancer site until my fifteenth anniversary. *(This time span has now been increased by the medical field.)*

My first chemotherapy was a terrible experience for me. Believing I could lick any problems it might cause by Biblical positive thinking, I was thrown for a loop when I suffered more than some other patients I knew at the time.

I have never had a sensitive stomach. Knowing I would not vomit, I then proceeded to set a new record for the *Guinness Book of World Records* (on the vomiting side, that is!).

All reports indicate that chemotherapy is continually being improved—as far as the side effects are concerned. I certainly found that to be true during my 1994 treatments. Therefore, my answer to one of the most-asked questions I hear remains, "Yes, without a doubt, I **would** take chemotherapy again."

No matter what treatment a person does or does not

choose to use, I am not to tell anyone else what to do. Neither do I need to judge why someone dies earlier than I think they need to die.

Often we think we have all the facts about people who did not take chemotherapy when we really did not have all the factors. Perhaps they knew it was no use to take chemotherapy in their case. They just didn't want to share the extent of their cancer with the world.

Let's just ask God to guide all cancer patients as they are told the catastrophic news, "It's cancer!"

"The steps of a good man are ordered by the LORD: and he delighteth in his way. Though he fall, he shall not be utterly cast down: for the LORD upholdeth him with his hand." (Psalms 37:23, 24)

CHAPTER TWENTY-TWO

ACCEPT HELP!

Y ES, ACCEPTING HELP **can** be humiliating, and, yes, it **can** cause a sense of obligation if you let it, and, yes, it **can** be misunderstood. But, if you don't learn to accept help, you are probably going to be more unusable than if you humble yourself and encourage those who will help you.

If it actually is more blessed to give than to receive, **and the Bible says it is**, then you are the cause of a person getting the better part of the deal by letting her give you help. *"I have shewed you all things, how that so labouring ye ought to support the weak, and to remember the words of the Lord Jesus, how he said, It is more blessed to give than to receive."* (Acts 20:35)

• A married student couple at Hyles-Anderson College wanted us to have a **full-course, home-cooked meal** every Thursday night. They told us they were going to do this for a year. I asked them not to promise something I felt would be difficult to maintain. They insisted and missed only once. And that time, they asked someone to fulfill what they felt was their responsibility. They brought the food whether or not I was sick or even at home. They made an arrangement about what to do if no one was at home at delivery time. Sometimes

169

we have had leftovers through the weekend from this Thursday night meal. This couple found ways to make this work without putting any responsibility on us. They even used aluminum foil containers to keep me from worrying about their dishes.

After a year, this couple left to start a church in Georgia, but not before they recruited others to take their place. We continue to have full-course, home-cooked meals brought to our house every Thursday evening. I cannot begin to explain what this means to my husband and me.

• A lady from our church comes to my house to dust, vacuum and do several things for several hours every Monday. She asks me every time I see her to leave notes for extras such as removing ashes from the fireplace or squeezing oranges for fresh juice. She has several ladies who help her each week. When one of the ladies assisting her moves away or has circumstances arise where she can no longer help, this lady finds a replacement. What a blessing to walk into a fresh-smelling, orderly clean house after a morning of teaching!

• Because of degenerative disc disease, I use a special tall chair that enables me to see over the podium when I teach. Young men see to it that this heavy, cumbersome chair is always in my classroom at class time. They don't wait to see if I need it on a particular day. It's just there. I might not need it or even want it. It's just there. How grateful I am for these young men taking time from their schedules to care for a lady old enough to be their grandmother!

So many diseases or post-operative problems are come and go. One hour you don't need something and the next hour you do. It's so much better to let a helper keep his routine scheduled task done than to say something like, "Oh, I didn't need that today." This paves the way for the responsibility not to be done the next day when it is needed desperately.

"We then that are strong ought to bear the infirmities of the weak and not to please ourselves." (Romans 15:1)

Churches Take Care of Me!

I am able to travel for *Christian Womanhood* and speak at mini-spectaculars quite easily because:

- I am not left in airports to sit long periods of time with my head balancing on my diseased neck (degenerative disc disease). Help is waiting for me because other helpers have arranged it.

- Someone from the *Christian Womanhood* staff meets me at each meeting to assist me personally, as well as help *Christian Womanhood* as an organization.

- The coordinator at each meeting has a recliner in the meeting place so that I can "get my head off my neck" while I enjoy other speakers.

- I am scheduled with breaks for rest in a nearby room at the church. The coordinators are so kind to outfit this room with a bed or a cot so that I can nap if I so desire (I usually do!).

What Do I Prefer?

You ask me if I prefer this help. The answer is, "No." I

prefer not having degenerative disc disease with its accompanying medicine, rest and treatment schedules. I would have preferred that I had not had several spinal operations over 20 years ago. I would have preferred not to have had cancer twice, cancer surgery twice, and chemotherapy twice with all its side effects.

However, God has not seen fit to give me my preferences about every little thing. God has been good to me. He has been good to me to give me the help I have needed whether or not I preferred it. No, I do not prefer to have help. I grew up a very active, physically strong person who preferred to give help to others. However, since I do prefer to be used of God through teaching, speaking and writing, I will continue to learn to accept help.

Of course, your needs will be completely individual depending on your age, condition of your health, and your present lifestyle; but, whatever your status, let others be used of God and be a blessing by making it easier for someone to help you. *"But I rejoiced in the Lord greatly, that now at the last your care of me hath flourished again; wherein ye were also careful, but ye lacked opportunity. Not that I speak in respect of want: for I have learned, in whatsoever state I am, therewith to be content."* (Philippians 4:10, 11)

CHAPTER TWENTY-THREE

WHEN SOMETHING DEVASTATING HAPPENS

M Y FORMER SUNDAY school teacher, Mrs. Olin Holbrook, often told us, "If you have never known sorrow and heartbreak, get ready, because your time will come." How right she was!

Eventually hard times come to every person's life, whether it is a wayward child, an illness such as cancer, the death of a loved one, a broken marriage, a church split, having someone you love disappoint you, or financial difficulties. How we respond to the hurts that come our way can be a testimony to the saved and unsaved alike.

Mrs. Olin Holbrook

Through the years, great Christians in my life, including

173

CANCER: MY ENEMY, MY FRIEND

Dr. Bob Jones, Sr., Dr. Lee Roberson, Dr. Jack Hyles and my husband, Dr. Wendell Evans, have helped me to learn the following principles for handling devastating news that comes to me.

- **Pour out your complaint unto God.** *"I cried unto the LORD with my voice; with my voice unto the LORD did I make my supplication. I poured out my complaint before him; I shewed before him my trouble."* (Psalms 142:1, 2)

- **Cry and commiserate with those closest, most confidential, and most understanding for a short while.** However, don't be surprised when you hear the news is being generally discussed. Bear in mind that very few people are able to keep information totally confidential.

- **Thank God for allowing good to come out of hurt.** I Thessalonians 5:18 says, *"In every thing give thanks: for this is the will of God in Christ Jesus concerning you."*

- **Plan your stance.** Plan what you are going to say and what you are going to leave unsaid. Plan who you are going to ask for help. Decide what you can learn from the situation. Decide how much you absolutely have to do in regard to the problem at the time.

- **Make your game plan to dilute the hurt.** Put away any reminders of the hurt for the immediate time. Busy yourself in caring for your personal needs. Refuse to allow your body to go without the right nourishment by saying, "I don't want to eat." That only makes you feel worse. Think of those things you need to do in order to keep your life on as even a keel as possible. Perhaps making a call to bring encouragement to someone else will help dilute your pain as you think on someone else's trouble.

- **Keep thanking God for the good things about the hurt if the hurt keeps coming back to mind.** For example, after a car accident, try to follow these steps:

  A. Always major on people who were not hurt, rather than on the damage to the vehicle or repair costs or insurance. Do not keep inspecting the damage.

  B. Think of the fact that more damage could have been done to the vehicles.

  C. Be grateful that you do not drink or take drugs which possibly kept matters from being worse. Thank God for the teaching and training you have received that helps you live a clean life.

  D. Be thankful your training caused you to obey your authorities and possess an up-to-date driver's license. *"Obey them that have the rule over you, and submit yourselves."* (Hebrews 13:17a)

  E. Make lists of other things for which to be thankful. Use "flip-side thinking" at its finest. ("Flip-Side Thinking" is chapter 23 in Marlene Evans' first book *Redbirds and Rubies and Rainbows* which teaches Biblical philosophies on life in a homespun, delightful way.)

175

- **Refuse to think out more than one step at a time when your mind wants to take care of everything at once.** By this time, the hurt might have caved in on you again. (Read Chapter 4 entitled "One Step at a Time" from *Redbirds and Rubies and Rainbows*.)

- **Once you have been able to get your mind off the hurt for a period of time, you can begin making necessary decisions without making imprudent statements you will regret.** How often I have seen people make decisions in the heat of a crisis and regret their hasty action for the rest of their lives. *"Be not rash with thy mouth, and let not thine heart be hasty to utter any thing before God: for God is in heaven, and thou upon earth: therefore let thy words be few."* (Ecclesiastes 5:2)

- **Ask God for answers to help you avoid the same type of hurt in the future, unless it is His perfect will to allow it in your life for His glory, as you learn to praise Him in all things.** *"It is good for me that I have been afflicted; that I might learn thy statues."* (Psalm 119:71)

Having a ready-made plan to meet any trouble that comes into our lives will help us go through the difficulties in a Spirit-controlled way. As I said before, the way in which we respond to our hurts can be a positive testimony to the saved and unsaved alike.

CHAPTER TWENTY-FOUR

THE WORD OF THE 90'S — COMFORTABLE

"**Y**OU SHOULDN'T DO this if you don't feel **comfortable** with it."

"Oh, you feel **comfortable** with that?"

"I feel so **comfortable** with that person. He makes me feel like a total woman."

"I am not going to take chemotherapy because I don't feel **comfortable** sitting with the other patients. I don't want to look like them."

These are examples of questions and statements I hear so often nowadays that reflect the current thinking of our society. I can't help but wonder how **comfortable** Jesus felt hanging from the cross for us? *"Then released he Barabbas unto them: and when he had scourged Jesus, he delivered him to be crucified. Then the soldiers of the governor took Jesus into the common hall, and gathered unto him the whole band of soldiers. And they stripped him, and put on him a scarlet robe. And when they had plaited a crown of thorns, they put* *it upon his head, and a reed in his right hand: and they bowed the knee before him, and mocked him, saying, Hail, King of the Jews! And they spit upon him, and took the reed, and smote him on the head. And after that they had mocked him, they took the robe off from him, and put his own raiment on him, and led him away to crucify him. And as they came out, they found a man of Cyrene, Simon by name: him they compelled to bear his cross. And when they were come unto a place called Golgotha, that is to say, a place of a skull, They gave him vinegar to drink mingled with gall: and when he had tasted thereof, he would not drink. And they crucified him, and parted his garments, casting lots: that it might be fulfilled which was spoken by the prophet, They parted my garments among them, and upon my vesture did they cast lots. And sitting down they watched him there; And set up over his head his accusation written, THIS IS JESUS THE KING OF THE JEWS."* (Matthew 27:26-37)

Jesus must have not felt too **comfortable** as He asked why His father had forsaken Him. *"And about the ninth hour Jesus cried with a loud voice, saying, Eli, Eli, lama sabach-tha-ni? that is to say, My God, my God, why hast thou forsaken me?"* (Matthew 27:46)

We often say that we want to be close to Jesus, and yet, at the same time, we want to be sure that our lives include all the material possessions we desire in order to be **comfortable**.

However, if we really want to know Him, we just might be called on to live out Philippians 3:10 which says, *"That I may know him, and the power of his resurrection, and the fellowship of his sufferings, being made conformable unto his death."*

We All Enjoy Being Comfortable

I'm sure there is nothing wrong with having those material possessions that make us **feel comfortable** if it is financially possible for us to have them. I happen to like my comfortable house. I like to have a comfortable chair and bed for times of rest and relaxation.

It's a great feeling to be around those people who make us feel **comfortable**. It's nice to feel **comfortable** with the requirements on the job. We sometimes call it "finding our niche." However, the world is going much further than that. Actually, the question, "Are you **comfortable** with that?" is fairly comparable to the old slogan, "If it feels good, do it."

Putting Comfort First
Will Eventually Ruin Us

In a world obsessed with comfort, we are likely to ruin our lives or, at least, make mistakes for time and eternity by choosing churches, schools and jobs where we feel **comfortable**. To tell you the truth, I might feel more **comfortable** in a teaching position where the teachers can say to the students, "Attend class if you want. We don't take roll. If you pass the test at the end of the semester, you receive your credits." That would take a lot of the business work out of teaching. But, it's scary to think of your surgeon having received his credits in such a fashion.

Comfortable Churches

Recently we have been receiving notices in the mail from several new "churches" in our area. They are advertising what amounts to be a new social club that has thrown in some kindness and love. Other areas of our country are seeing the same thing happen. The ads go something like this:

- Dress as you like!
- An alternative to the traditional church!
- Believe what you like!
- Come when you can!

Biblical beliefs, standards and thinking are all but absolved except for love and kindness. Other than violence and murder, sin is not mentioned. Because the whole Bible is not preached, sin is only that with which you do not feel comfortable. The thinking that all guilt is bad is also touted in this "comfort-driven" society. I have not seen any soul winning suggested. Do you suppose they think if they are kind, people around them will learn how to go to Heaven? It reminds me of the old "modernism," now called "liberalism," with a slightly different flair.

Drive-Ins Have Led to Drive-Through Churches

Church-going folks can salve their consciences even more quickly with the latest "people-friendly churches." Drive-in churches have now led to drive-through churches in some areas. You can watch a 12-minute "religious" video as you drive through one place about which I recently read in the newspaper.

The church is trying as fast as it can to be a gigantic social club, and it appears the more **comfortable** the churches become, the more discontent the people are and the worse the world becomes. People may think they are looking for comfort when, in reality, they are looking for truth and the peace of God. Sad to say, these new churches looming on the horizon do not give truth and the peace of God.

Don't Get So Comfortable
You Miss Peace of Mind

I hope you can have some comforts of life, but don't get so **comfortable** that you or those around you don't know anything about the fact, *"That I may know him, and the power of his resurrection, and the fellowship of his sufferings, being made conformable unto his death."* (Philippians 3:10) Though doing so may require us to give up a few or sometimes many of our comforts, knowing Him will give you peace of mind that counts far more than comfort.

Some Times
I Haven't Felt Comfortable

There have been many times in my life when I have not felt **comfortable**—from the time I was a young child and on through every stage of my life, including the present. Let me share some of my uncomfortable times:

• Learning to tie my own shoes

• Entering college 1,200 miles away from home... and staying

• Not leaving college to go home and care for my mother when the news of her mastectomy came

• Back surgery and the long recovery

- Being studied by the state of Tennessee in order to adopt our children

- Telling people how Jesus' blood could change their destination from Hell to Heaven

- Being corrected

- Taking chemotherapy—twice

Needless to say, I could add many other circumstances, but just the examples of staying out of my comfort area that I have listed have given me much benefit. I have observed over and over that people who accomplish much of anything in life have to do some stretching, and stretching isn't always **comfortable**. Reject the word of the 90's—**comfortable**— *"For Christ also hath once suffered for sins, the just for the unjust, that he might bring us to God, being put to death in the flesh, but quickened by the Spirit."* (I Peter 3:18)

You may wonder what being **comfortable** has to do with my cancer book. It has not been **comfortable** to fight two battles with cancer, have cancer surgeries, and have two regimens of chemotherapy. It may seem that I was **comfortable** because I had people who cared for me. However, there were many times when people brought me no comfort. I had to decide to be *uncomfortable* to live.

CHAPTER TWENTY-FIVE

LIVING WITH DISAPPOINTMENT

P EOPLE OF ALL ages seem to live with disappointment much of their lives. If you live a life characterized by disappointment, you are probably setting yourself up for even greater times of disappointment in those years that are supposed to be the "golden years."

I want to share some thoughts with you that I have had as I listened to my preacher, Dr. Jack Hyles. These thoughts are not direct quotes but statements that I wrote down right after hearing Brother Hyles one Sunday. His statements provoked my thinking about living with cancer or any other difficulty that comes my way.

• **Don't set yourself up for disappointment because disappointment leads to hurt.** Hurt leads to anger, anger leads to wrath, and wrath leads to evil. Allowing yourself to be set up for disappointment can cause you to be bitter against those you love and cause you to mistreat them. Quite possibly your disappointment will cause you to say unkind words that can forever hurt or even ruin a relationship.

When we plan how people will respond to us through our cancer (or other hurts), we are opening ourselves up for hurt feelings. This is not fair to your loved ones, your friends or to yourself.

• **Disappointments come because your plans didn't work out.** Of course, after my ten year anniversary of being cancer-free and the doctor saying, "Why are you here? You are considered cured," I was somewhat tempted to not plan on having cancer again. However, because I didn't put my weight down on my oncologist's words, I wasn't too surprised when the second diagnosis of cancer came. When we make our own plans, we are setting ourselves up to have to work through disappointments.

• **Let God make the arrangements.** *"Go to now, ye that say, To day or to morrow we will go into such a city, and continue there a year, and buy and sell, and get gain: Whereas ye know not what shall be on the morrow. For what is your life? It is even a vapour, that appeareth for a little time, and then vanisheth away. For that ye ought to say, If the Lord will, we shall live, and do this, or that."* (James 4:13-15)

• **Disappointments equal being deprived of some arrangement.** I believe that God can miraculously heal if He chooses to do so. However, it is possible that for my good and His glory He might not choose to heal me. If I get my mind so set on a complete, miraculous healing I am setting myself up to be deprived of what I think I should have.

• **Don't make too many plans, appointments or arrangements that can go wrong.** Live life one step at a time.

- **Don't plan how something is going to be.** I thought I wasn't going to vomit during my first regimen of chemotherapy. That expectation was short-lived as I found myself in the bathroom losing my first good meal!

- **Don't have a lot of expectations.** I must admit I had a good number of expectations as I went into my first chemotherapy. I had no idea how many of my personal expectations for myself would never be realized. In the same way, don't have a lot of expectations for others—what they are going to do for you, when they will come to visit you, how they will treat you, and so forth. You **will** be disappointed.

Let's let these seven little statements work in our lives to help us have a contented happy life, rather than a life filled with disappointments.

CHAPTER TWENTY-SIX

MAKE EVERY DAY
A CHRISTMAS DAY!

"**M**AKE EVERY DAY a Christmas Day" is certainly not a new thought to me, and probably it is not to you either, but it definitely has had new meaning to me this past year. I'd like for you to think it through again with me. Perhaps you've always wanted to follow this advice, but you haven't taken steps to do so.

The incident that happened which especially brought this thought to my attention at this time was a visit with my coordinating doctor at Mayo Clinic. Our family has been with him many years; therefore, he was glad to see Joy with me on my last Mayo visit before Joy was to return with her husband and children to the mission field. Dr. Frigas was very interested in their missionary work in Papua New Guinea.

I had been trying to prepare Joy to go back to New Guinea with the thought that she could put me and my future with this ovarian cancer into the hands of God. I wanted her to be able to give herself to her family and her work. Forgetting that Dr. Frigas was from Greece and that he had a mother and a father die in the past few years, I mentioned to him that I was wanting to help my daughter get ready to leave the country.

I realized that Dr. Frigas was certainly the very one to philosophize with Joy when he reminded me that he had to leave his sick mother in the hands of others in a poorer country, even though he himself was in the United States with a support group of two thousand doctors, 15,000 other medical personnel, and all the latest medical machines. He also had and still has immediate access to new medicines the very day the Federal Drug Administration approves one.

Not only that, he knew that when his last parent died, the poor people from Albania would come invade his family home and take everything of value before the body of his parent would be discovered. That did happen, and Dr. Frigas took the attitude that the things that were taken would do some good for the poor people. He was rejoicing about the fact that some of the most sentimental things, like pictures that would be important only to his sister and himself, were not stolen. He could more than relate to Joy's situation.

He almost apologized for Christmas being such a big event in their culture, but he went on to explain that each time he returned home to visit his family, they made every moment they had together during the years his parents were sick a Christmas Day! As he challenged Joy to do that with me in the days she had remaining here in the United States, I so wanted her to take his advice and put her mind on her work and her family as she prepared to go back to the bush country. I know she's in a tough situation. What news she does receive about me will have to be radioed to her from a town that has a telephone.

MAKE EVERY DAY A CHRISTMAS DAY!

I really believe that Joy took Dr. Frigas' advice to heart, and I'm suggesting you do some of the things I'm going to mention she has done. Don't wait until there's a life-threatening illness before you decide to make every day a Christmas Day.

• **Joy never came into the house or left the house without saying, "You precious mama," or "I love you."** It is so important to verbalize your sentiments and love to those closest to you. *"A word spoken in due season how good it is."* (Proverbs 15:23b)

• **If Joy saw that I needed quiet time more than I needed her company, she quickly arranged for that without seeming to feel rejection at all.** Watch for the needs of those around you and work at giving them exactly what they need rather than what you want to give them at that time. Claim Psalm 119:165 which says, *"Great peace have they which love thy law, and nothing shall offend them,"* to help keep your hurt feelings "at bay."

• **Joy let me into her life, and I do know some of the problems of a family of five adjusting to the winter months of the United States after coming from the jungle. She did not, however, bring up unnecessary worries that would so play on my mind.** Anyone with a weakened immune system (a result of sickness or chemotherapy) will readily admit that it is very easy to think negative thoughts and to always think that the worst will happen. Therefore, it is helpful for the sick person to not have unnecessary negative situations brought to their attention.

• **Though Joy was living in the missionary apartments provided by our preacher and church, she often ran in and** out of our house when we were not home, leaving her touch behind her. She could turn down my bed and have it all ready with my resting clothes laid out in a way that left her mark. Find simple, creative ways to "leave your mark" even when you have just a small amount of time to do a thoughtful deed. This lets the person know you have taken the time to think of them while you are apart.

• **Joy asked everyone she could ask to pray for me. She also left specific people with special responsibilities that they feel they have been asked to fulfill in her name.** I fear that we often underestimate the power of prayer. God does hear and answer prayer, and it is wise to enlist others to pray with you. When you cannot be there for someone you love, find others who can represent you and do things "in your name." This will surely help ease some of the guilt you might experience if you simply leave things undone.

• **Joy let the people who work around me know that she appreciated what they were able to do for me, when perhaps she could not do that thing even while she was home.** When one cannot do or be there for someone she loves, it is very easy to become jealous toward those who are able to be there. Find ways to say thank you to these people to help keep your own spirit right and healthy. Thank God for the people He has sent when you cannot physically be there. *"In every thing give thanks: for this is the will of God in Christ Jesus concerning you."* (I Thessalonians 5:18)

• **When Joy had good reports about anybody or anything, she saw to it that she got them to me as quickly as possible.** Keep your eyes and ears open for good things to tell those you love. These may be some good words or things you have heard about them or others. Be an encourager.

- **Even with seeing to it that she did not neglect her husband and three small children (9, 6, 4), Joy tried her best to work her schedule in a way where she could run errands for me and work around what I needed.** Sometimes running an errand for what seems to be the smallest item may really be a big deal for the person in need. For example, going to pick up a cup of soup at a local restaurant for me may have seemed insignificant to some, but with the chemotherapy my appetite was quite small. Very few things tasted good to me, and therefore, sometimes something like a cup of soup was truly a big deal to me.

- **If Joy and the family were planning to come over to the house one day and they saw that it had been an especially hard day for me, she would say, "You don't need us over here," when I knew she wanted to spend every bit of time possible with me while she was home.** However, by doing this, Joy received better time with me later. Had she and her family come when I was unable to give myself to them in a way they would feel welcome and loved, it would not only have possibly caused hurt feelings at that time, but it would have prevented me from getting the rest I needed in order to be better the next time Joy came. She was, in essence, exchanging quantity for quality.

- **Joy has seemingly built on all the good that happened to her in our home, and she has blocked anything that I did wrong, so that it seems she has her husband loving me every bit as much as she does.** Because no one is perfect but Jesus, all parents make mistakes in rearing their children. However, Joy never seems to remember any of my mistakes. She simply majors on all the good times we had during her growing up years and shares those with Jeff, thereby giving him a good mindset toward me.

- **Joy lifted my spirits and shared her love to me through the medium of prose.** I want to share her heart-touching words which she wrote while still in Papua New Guinea. She had received word of my cancer and impending surgery, and my prognosis was very bleak. *"As cold waters to a thirsty soul, so is good news from a far country."* (Proverbs 25:25)

My First Thoughts About Mom When I Received Word that She Might Not Live Through Surgery
April 16, 1994, 8:00 P.M.
Maprik, Papua New Guinea

Her laughter... loud, contagious,
boisterous, giving, loving, from the gut.
Her tears...
Jordan says she cries about everything.
What can I learn?
How can I give back? What can I give?
Her wisdom... unbelievable,
such common sense, knows people.
Her unselfish love...always giving,
looking for ways to please people,
her family, her son, husband, grandkids, daughter,
daughter-in-law, son-in-law.
Always has great ideas.
I picture her grave by a tree—
a big shady one.
Her love of redbirds...
passed on to others, including me.
I'll never look at another mountain
or tree the same again.

MAKE EVERY DAY A CHRISTMAS DAY!

Her love of people...
the hurting people and wanting to help them.
Her submissiveness to Daddy.
Her willingness to accept the things
she cannot change.
Always helping to grow...
showing me ways to grow, mature.
Always helping me to get the family traditions
I hold dear...
making them come true for me,
moving mountains if she had to.
Giving always!!
Her love of nature...birds, trees, animals —
our trip to Yellowstone!
Don't die in pain, Momma.
How can I soak up all your wisdom?
Wisdom comes from God...
so you would tell me to go to God
and listen to my preacher.
God is Sovereign!!
I wish you didn't have to suffer, Momma...
there's no one like you.
Do you know my love for you?
My thankfulness?
Your love of God and the Bible.
Will I ever use a Flair marking pen again
without thinking of her?!

— Joy Evans Ryder

I hope these very personal examples will give you lots of
ideas to help you make every day a Christmas Day.

CHAPTER TWENTY-SEVEN

"I DON'T DO..."

MANY LADIES WHO clean houses professionally let it be known in advance that they don't do windows. "I don't do windows," is a standard answer for not being willing to do deep cleaning.

I wonder how many Christians ought to warn the unsaved, fellow Christians, and even God that they don't do soul winning. If Christians in fundamental, soul-winning Baptist churches don't do soul winning, who will tell people how to go to Heaven when they die? I have to be honest, when I was under the effects of chemotherapy and trying to heal from surgery, I had many days when I wanted to put up a big banner that read, **"I DON'T DO NOTHIN'!!"** And that surely would have included telling anyone how to go to Heaven when they die.

But even when we are well, I am afraid we are quick to make statements such as:
"I **do** typing."
"I **do** decorations."
"I **do** cooking for the bereaved."
"I **do** hospital visitation."
"I **do** giving."

195

CANCER: MY ENEMY, MY FRIEND

I am afraid we are even pretty quick (relatively speaking) to say:
"I **do** Sunday school teaching."
"I **do** daily vacation Bible school."
"I **do** choir."

And even:
"I **do** the Bible."
"I **do** prayer."

And would you believe:
"I **do** church bus work."

But, for all practical purposes, most Christians ought to just declare: "I **don't do** soul winning."

If you feel you no longer want to say, "I don't do soul winning," please learn this plan, use it today, and look for opportunities to use it the rest of your life.

In I John 5:13, the Bible says, *"These things have I written unto you that believe on the name of the Son of God: that ye may know that ye have eternal life."* You can **know** you are on your way to Heaven.

In Romans 3:10, the Bible says, *"As it is written, There is none righteous, no, not one,* and in verse 23, *"For all have sinned, and come short of the glory of God."* These verses mean that everyone sins, and that means you are a sinner, also.

In Romans 5:12a, the Bible tells us from where sin came: *"Wherefore, as by one man sin entered into the world and death by sin; and so **death** passed upon all men, for that all*

196

have sinned." This means Adam committed the first sin in the whole world. This word, "death," doesn't mean just dying and going to the grave; it means eternal separation from God in a lake of fire. This is our punishment for our sin and a debt you owe as of right now.

But, thankfully, the story doesn't end there! In Romans 6:23, the Bible says, *"For the wages of sin is death; but the **gift** of God is eternal life through Jesus Christ our Lord."* Going to Heaven is a gift; it's absolutely free!

If you know that you're a sinner, you realize there is a penalty for that sin, you can't pay for it yourself, and you realize that Jesus died on the cross and shed His blood for your sins, this is what you need to do. In Romans 10:9 and 13, the Bible says, *"That if thou shalt confess with thy mouth the Lord Jesus, and shalt believe in thine heart that God hath raised him from the dead, thou shalt be saved. For **whosoever** shall call upon the name of the Lord shall be saved."* "Whosoever" means you. We could put your name in the blanks: "For ___ shall call upon the name of the Lord and ___ shall be saved."

If you will trust Jesus to take you to Heaven when you die, pray this prayer: "Dear Jesus, forgive me of my sins. I trust You today, Jesus, and only You to take me to Heaven when I die. Thank You for saving me. Amen."

According to the Bible, if you were to die today, you would go to Heaven because in John 3:36 the Bible says, *"He that believeth on the Son **hath** everlasting life."*

Let me give you some ways to **do** soul winning:

- Ask someone to go with you.

- Commit to a specific time to go weekly and stick to that time. It seems the devil will throw anything possible at us to interfere with the time we are to use telling others about Jesus.

- Memorize the verses to the plan of salvation. Mark them in a purse-sized New Testament and carry it with you all the time.

- Carry tracts with you that you can leave with people if you do not have the opportunity to give the entire plan of salvation.

- Take advantage of every opportunity possible to tell someone about Christ, such as waiting in the doctor's office, while paying salespersons, and while waiting for someone at the mall. The list of opportunities is endless.

- Ask God for boldness, strength and Holy Spirit power to help you do His work.

"And he (Jesus) *said unto them, Go ye into all the world, and preach the gospel to every creature."* (Mark 16:15)

There is not a better thing to do than to find a way to tell others how to go to Heaven. I guarantee that it will take your mind off your sickness and yourself.

EPILOGUE
by
Marlene Evans

CHAPTER TWENTY-EIGHT

I'VE DECIDED TO LIVE UNTIL I DIE!

W ITH ALL THE statistics, materials, and even hopeful new treatments being reported for ovarian cancer, Stage IV, I read that a two to three year survival rate after diagnosis is considered a big victory. Now I know that God can take care of all the statistics and choose to work a direct miracle if He so desires. I also know God uses the minds of people to discover new medicines.

However, I'd be lying to tell you that I am not thinking about preparing to leave this earth. We all need to be doing that anyway, so I can't lose if I'm "gettin' ready to leave this world."

As I've gone back and forth the last one and one-half years about the statistics if a patient has surgery or doesn't have surgery, the timing of surgery, taking chemotherapy, and the kinds of chemotherapy, I have sometimes become quite confused. Do I die two and one-half years from the time the cancer started growing, from diagnosis, or from treatment?

This consequently caused me to be confused about some other things. For example, I needed new orthopedic shoes and since they are quite expensive, I wasn't sure I should spend the money on new ones. I hated to spend the money on new shoes if I wouldn't wear them very long. This thinking, I realized, was beginning to hinder me in several areas of my life. However, one good day (sometime in February 1995), I was struck by a brilliant idea. **I'LL JUST LIVE UNTIL I DIE.** Here's the way my reasoning went.

1. Living until I die is all I have ever been able to do with or without cancer.

2. Even if I die physically, I won't die.

3. Until I do go from this earth (ten minutes or ten years from now), I would like to live while I'm still breathing.

4. As the old saying goes, "It's not over till it's over," and more importantly, according to Romans 8:35-39, I can be a conqueror through death or life. *"Who shall separate us from the love of Christ? shall tribulation, or distress, or persecution, or famine, or nakedness, or peril, or sword? As it is written, For thy sake we are killed all the day long; we are accounted as sheep for the slaughter. Nay, in all these things we are more than conquerors through him that loved us. For I am persuaded, that neither death, nor life, nor angels, nor principalities, nor powers, nor things present, nor things to come, Nor height, nor depth, nor any other creature, shall be able to separate us from the love of God, which is in Christ Jesus our Lord."*

5. Many people (even young people) seem dead while they are still breathing. I've had a lot of living I've been able

to do.

6. I don't ever want to die. God, in His goodness and wisdom, figured out a way for me just to go from life to life with works following after me. Yes, since I believe Romans 10:9 which says, *"That if thou shalt confess with thy mouth the Lord Jesus, and shalt believe in thine heart that God hath raised him from the dead, thou shalt be saved, "* and since I'm not depending on myself for Heaven, I'll just go from life to life. *"For by grace are ye saved through faith; and that not of yourselves: it is the gift of God: Not of works, lest any man should boast. "* (Ephesians 2:8, 9)

By winning souls to Christ *("Go ye therefore, and teach all nations, baptizing them in the name of the Father, and of the Son, and of the Holy Ghost: Teaching them to observe all things whatsoever I have commanded you: and, lo, I am with you alway, even unto the end of the world." [Matthew 28:19-20])* and helping others *("Then shall he answer them, saying, Verily I say unto you, Inasmuch as ye did it not to one of the least of these, ye did it not to me." [Matthew 25:45])*, my works will follow after me according to Revelation 14:13 which says, *"And I heard a voice from heaven saying unto me, Write, Blessed are the dead which die in the Lord from henceforth: Yea, saith the Spirit, that they may rest from their labours; and their works do follow after them. "*

7. But, the nagging question comes. How will I die? I do not know, but whatever I go through, Jesus will go through it with me because He promises in Hebrews 13:5, *"Let your conversation be without covetousness; and be content with such things as ye have: for he hath said, I will never leave thee, nor forsake thee. "*

Since I'm going to Heaven when I stop breathing, *("Let not your heart be troubled: ye believe in God, believe also in me. In my Father's house are many mansions: if it were not so, I would have told you. I go to prepare a place for you. And if I go to prepare a place for you, I will come again, and receive you unto myself; that where I am, there ye may be also. And whither I go ye know, and the way ye know."* [John 14:1-4]), I might as well plan on nothing but life.

Are There Ever Times I Feel Differently?

Yes! Those times come when I let negative thoughts stay in my mind — keeping bats in my belfry!

1. False pride tells me I cannot do what I could do before surgery and chemotherapy. Actually, I really am aware God could choose to take one thing I do and bless it above all I've ever done. *"And Samson said, Let me die with the Philistines. And he bowed himself with all his might; and the house fell upon the lords, and upon all the people that were therein. So the dead which he slew at his death were more than they which he slew in his life."* (Judges 16:30) My flesh causes me to forget that He (through me) does anything I do anyway.

2. Fighting side effects of surgery, treatment, a low immune system, etc., causes me to think on myself, declaring myself a hypochondriac. I sometimes feel sorry for myself when the back gets help and something else begins to give trouble. I Thessalonians 5:18 which says, *"In every thing give thanks: for this is the will of God in Christ Jesus concerning you,"* can soon care for that pity party.

3. False pride tells me I can't do what others can do. I have been warned about that in II Corinthians 10:12 which says, *"For we dare not make ourselves of the number, or compare ourselves with some that commend themselves: but they measuring themselves by themselves, and comparing themselves among themselves, are not wise."*

4. False pride tells me that my Papua New Guinea grandchildren will remember a sick, weak, no-fun grandma, as I was still in treatment when they left to return to the mission field.

Playing with the grandkids at McDonald's

I get out of these feelings when I start doing what I can do now. Preparing a fun box of school supplies for those Papua New Guinea grandkids is a lot better for my health than worrying about what I couldn't be when they were here.

The fact is, I'm awake and evidently not needing sleep or I wouldn't be aware enough to think the negative thoughts. I try to turn myself back over to God, make a short cheery call, or do something else I can do, and I'm on my way out of the depths of despair.

You are, no doubt, in a different situation, age or position from mine, but what part of what I have written could you apply to your life?

YOUNG MOTHER, could you stop your busyness, simplify your lifestyle, go out to the sandpile, and really live a few minutes with and for your child?

SINGLE MOM, could you set up a "T" and play with your young son instead of dying a little every day over the fact that there is no on-site dad?

WIFE OF ANY AGE, could you leave your world and enter the world of your husband for a few minutes—not just doing for him but living (really living) with him?

SUNDAY SCHOOL TEACHER, could you think on your lesson every day until God gives you something special to cause your class to live next Sunday?

CHURCH BUS ROUTE WORKER, could you pick up a pretty shell for everyone on your route the next time you are on vacation? You would live a little more and so would the riders.

Let's all live until we die!